**Bush
Theatre**

G000255836

Headlong and the Bush Theatre present the UK premiere of

BOYS WILL BE BOYS

by Melissa Bubnic

25 June – 30 July 2016

Bush Hall, London

Boys Will Be Boys was originally commissioned by
Sydney Theatre Company and first produced at the Wharf 2 Theatre
by Sydney Theatre Company on 16th April 2015

BOYS WILL BE BOYS

by Melissa Bubnic

Cast

(in order of appearance)

Astrid Wentworth	**Kirsty Bushell**
Priya Sengupta	**Ellora Torchia**
Isabelle	**Chipo Chung**
Harrison Stevenson	**Emily Barber**
Arthur Beale	**Helen Schlesinger**
Pianist	**Jennifer Whyte**

Creative Team

Director	**Amy Hodge**
Designer	**Joanna Scotcher**
Lighting Designer	**Lee Curran**
Sound Designer	**Emma Laxton**
Musical Director	**James Fortune**
Movement Director	**Sarah Dowling**
Fight Director	**Ruth Cooper-Brown of RC-ANNIE Ltd**
Assistant Director	**Poppy Rowley**
Costume Supervisor	**Claire Wardroper**
Casting Director	**Lotte Hines**
Production Manager	**Simon Evans**
Assistant Production Manager	**Aubrey Turner**
Production Sound Engineer	**Jamie McIntyre**
Company Stage Manager	**Alicia White**
Assistant Stage Manager	**Amy Slater**
Stage Management placement	**Seana Green**

Headlong and the Bush Theatre would like to thank Alex Gilbreath, Jennifer Jackson, Clare Perkins, Rachel Redford, Beatriz Romilly, Charmian Hoare, Adam and Shane at The Rigging Team, Rohanna Eade, Temitope Ajose-Cutting, Elspeth Morrison, Rohanna Eade, Nic Donithorn, House of Fraser.

Boys Will Be Boys is supported by MA Dramatic Writing at Drama Centre London at Central Saint Martins.

A Note from the Author

In 2011, Sydney Theatre Company asked for my take on recent scandals in the Royal Australian Navy. A cadet who had complained to the police about being filmed during intercourse without her consent was made to apologise to her year level for bringing the Navy into disrepute. Another cadet didn't realise she had been raped until she was told by colleagues of the explicit footage her rapist had taken during the act. I was intrigued by these incidents, among many others. This play isn't about misogyny (although of course, there's plenty of misogyny in it). It's not about why some men hate, but about what the women who are in these environments have to do to survive.

Boys Will Be Boys is a play about how women navigate sex and power in a man's world. Why the City? Because like the Navy, it's a domain where extremes intersect – a 'work hard, play hard' culture of extreme masculinity. It also oozes wealth and privilege, and for me, had more dramatic playfulness than the confines of a boat. I'm not suggesting that the events of the play are typical of all City workers. It's a vast industry and some of the insiders I met claimed to have no knowledge of the behaviours and attitudes found in the play, and argued that such a view of the City is outdated. And some insiders shared experiences of such extreme sexism and racism that I couldn't write it, because it was too outrageous to be believable. How can women thrive in a place where someone's idea of corporate hospitality is a lap dance and VIP treatment at a boutique brothel?

According to neuroscientist Joe Herbert, in a man-made world '[women] either become surrogate men... or you change the world'. Astrid Wentworth has chosen to become a surrogate man. Some claim that stripping and prostitution empowers women, that these are activities of sexual liberation. Astrid goes to strip clubs, uses prostitutes and out-alphas the most alpha male not because it's empowering but because she does not consider herself a woman (something weak and second-class), but a man who sits to pee. But Astrid needs to perform both man and woman simultaneously – she can objectify naked women, but she still better look sexy as fuck while doing so. A woman who isn't hot has no value at all. Women have to do everything men can do, but backwards and in heels.

The title is obviously a provocation, an aphorism used to excuse bad male behaviour as only natural. But are there behaviours that are 'natural' to men and women? The fact that women play the roles of men indicates my own belief that gender is a performance, a performance we may have learned so well that it feels natural to us, but a performance nonetheless. And because it's learned behaviour and not biology, such behaviours can change, adapt.

If acting like a surrogate man is the key to Astrid's success, then it is also the reason for her downfall. You can't win at a game where the rules are rigged against you. Only by dismantling the system entirely and building it anew, or as Joe Herbert says, 'you change the world', do women stand any chance at equality.

Melissa Bubnic
June 2016

Cast and Crew

Kirsty Bushell (Astrid Wentworth)
Kirsty Bushell returns to the Bush Theatre to play Astrid in *Boys Will Be Boys* – she previously appeared in *Disgraced* and *2000 Feet Away*. Kirsty last performed for Headlong in *Angels in America*. Her other theatre work includes *Hedda Gabler* (Salisbury Playhouse); *Antigone* (Barbican/tour); *The White Devil, Twelfth Night, The Comedy of Errors, The Tempest* (RSC); *The Big Meal* (Theatre Royal Bath); *Edward II, New Views 13, Edgar and Annabel, There is a War, Danton's Death, The Voysey Inheritance, Two Gentlemen of Verona* (National Theatre); *I Know How I Feel About Eve* (Hampstead); *Belongings* (West End/Hampstead); *1000 Stars Explode in the Sky, Don Juan* (Lyric Hammersmith); *Pornography* (Tricycle); *Serious Money* (Birmingham Rep); *Plenty, Far Away, Fen, A Girl in the Goldfish Bowl* (Sheffield Theatres); *Blue Heart, Testing the Echo* (Out of Joint); *The Seagull* (Northampton Theatres) and *An Inspector Calls* (West End). For television, her work includes *Silk, Frankie, Silent Witness, True Love, Roger Roger, EastEnders, Family Man* (BBC); *Injustice, FM* (ITV); *Pornography* (Channel 4); *Pulling* (Silver River/BBC); *Law & Order* (Kudos); *Midsomer Murders* (Bentley Productions); *Talk to Me* (Company Pictures) and *Life Isn't All Ha Ha Hee Hee* (Hat Trick). Film includes *Really* and *Women and Children*.

Ellora Torchia (Priya Sengupta)
Ellora Torchia's theatre credits include Out of Joint's production of *Macbeth*, directed by Max Stafford-Clark. Ellora's television credits include *Beowulf* (ITV); *Indian Summers* (New Pictures/Channel 4); *DCI Banks, The Suspicions of Mr Whicher – Beyond the Pale* (ITV) and *Spooks* (BBC). For film she has appeared in *Cowboys* (Pathé).

Chipo Chung (Isabelle)
Chipo Chung's theatre credits include *The Haunting of Hill House* (Liverpool Playhouse); *The Maids* (Harare International Festival of the Arts); *Fu Manchu* (Ovalhouse); *Phédre* (National Theatre); *Turandot* (Hampstead); *Fallujah* (Old Truman Brewery); *The Overwhelming* (National Theatre/Out of Joint); *Talking to Terrorists* (Out of Joint/Royal Court); *The Lunatic Queen* (Riverside Studios); *Tall Phoenix* (Belgrade); *Ma Rainey's Black Bottom* (Liverpool Playhouse); *The Mayor of Zalamea* (Liverpool Everyman) and *Hamlet* (Nuffield). Her television credits include *Thirteen, From Darkness, AD: Kingdom and Empire, Fortitude, The Politician's Husband, Sherlock, Camelot, Identity, Casualty, Doctor Who, Last Enemy, Holby City, Dr Who* and *Dalziel and Pascoe*. Chipo's film credits include *The White Room, 360, In the Loop, Sunshine* and *Proof*.

Emily Barber (Harrison Stevenson)
Emily graduated in 2014 from Royal Welsh College of Music & Drama.

Theatre credits include *Cymbeline* (Shakespeare's Globe); *The Importance of Being Earnest* (West End); *Billy Liar* (Royal Exchange, Manchester) and *Cornelius* (Finborough/59e59, New York). Short film includes *The Arrival* and *Burger* (Sundance Film Festival Winner). Radio includes *Sapper Dorothy*. Awards: Manchester Theatre Awards Best Newcomer 2014; Ian Charleson Nomination 2015.

Helen Schlesinger (Arthur Beale)
Helen Schlesinger's theatre credits include *Frozen* (Park); *Single Spies* (Rose); *Coriolanus* (Donmar Warehouse); *Bracken Moor* (Tricycle); *Fireface* (Young Vic); *Skåne*, *The Gods Weep*, *Comfort Me With Apples* (Hampstead); *Blue/Orange* (Arcola); *The Stone*, *Wild East*, *Bear Hug*, *The Weather* (Royal Court); *Whipping It Up* (Bush/Ambassadors); *The Crucible* (RSC/Gielgud); *Uncle Vanya*, *A Moon for the Misbegotten*, *King Lear*, *The Illusion*, *The Road to Mecca* (Royal Exchange, Manchester); *The Merchant of Venice*, *Twelfth Night* (RSC); *The Oresteia*, *War and Peace*, *Inadmissible Evidence* (National Theatre); *An Inspector Calls* (National Theatre/Garrick) and *Mill on the Floss* (Shared Experience). For film her work includes *Dirty War*, *24 Hour Party People* and *Persuasion*. For television, her work includes *Midsomer Murders*, *Lewis*, *The Hour*, *Merlin*, *Nativity*, *Criminal Justice*, *Trial and Retribution*, *Waking the Dead*, *Sensitive Skin*, *EastEnders*, *The Way We Live Now*, *Bad Girls*, *The Greatest Store in the World*, *The Cormorant* and *Bad Girl*.

Jennifer Whyte (Pianist)
Jennifer studied music at Glasgow University and the University of Massachusetts.

Her theatre credits as conductor/pianist include *Betty Blue Eyes*, *Les Misérables*, *Avenue Q*, *Follies*, *The Wiz*, *The Threepenny Opera*, *Cats*, *Sunset Boulevard*, *My Fair Lady*, *Whistle Down the Wind*, *The Phantom of the Opera*, *Martin Guerre*, *Show Boat* and *Dames at Sea*. Her credits as a composer for theatre include *Shehallion*, a Celtic music and dance show, *The Famished Land*, an Irish folk musical drama, and *Chasing Fate*, a gritty urban musical co-written with disadvantaged teenagers. Her newest piece for theatre is an American jazz musical called *Orville in the Underworld.*

Most recently she was on-set pianist for the movie version of *Les Misérables* at Pinewood Studios, associate musical director for *The Magistrate* at the Royal National Theatre and she has just recorded her first solo album of piano music for *Mozart Records.*

Melissa Bubnic (Playwright)
Melissa Bubnic is a writer for stage and screen. Her plays include *Boys Will Be Boys* (Headlong and Bush Theatre, Sydney Theatre Company); *Beached* (Marlowe Theatre and Soho Theatre, Melbourne Theatre Company, and Griffin Theatre Company); *Mariage Blanc* (Sydney Theatre Company) and *Stop. Rewind.* (Red Stitch Actors' Theatre, 2010, 2012). She won the Patrick White Award for *Beached* in 2010. She is currently writer-in-residence at the Orange Tree Theatre.

Amy Hodge (Director)
Amy Hodge is Creative Associate for Headlong. Her directing credits include *7-75* (The Place); *Am I Dead Yet?* (Unlimited/Traverse/Bush Theatre); *Our Big Land* (Romany Theatre Company); *The Rover* (Hampton Court Palace); *Romeo and Juliet* (Theatre Uz, Uzbekistan, for the British Council); *Clytemnestra*, *The Sanger*, *Light Arrested*, *Measure for Measure*, *A Christmas Carol*, *Small Change* (Sherman Cymru, while Associate Director 2008–2011); *Cloak Room* (Sherman /Washington DC); *Playing the Game* (Tricycle); *Mules* (Young Vic); *The Ethics of Progress* (Unlimited); *The Tempest*, *Kick for Touch* (Orange Tree) and *Change?* (West Yorkshire Playhouse). Amy was Studio Associate at the National Theatre (2013–14) and was recipient of the Jerwood Directors Award 2007.

Joanna Scotcher (Designer)

Joanna Scotcher received the WhatsOnStage 'Best Set Designer' Award for her site-specific design of *The Railway Children*, which went on to win the Olivier Award for Best Entertainment in 2011. Joanna was trained at the Royal Shakespeare Company. From this classical initiation in stage design, her design projects have taken her from performances on lakes, through journeys under forgotten London, to games in Royal Palaces. As well as her theatrical stage design, her work specialises in the world of immersive performance and site-responsive design, inhabiting spaces from the intimate to the epic.

Her design work has been exhibited at the V&A Museum's 'From Gaga to Gormley' exhibition and she has had installations commissioned by places such as Kensington Palace and Covent Garden. Recent work includes *Cuttin' It* (Young Vic/Royal Court/Birmingham Rep); *The Rolling Stone* (Orange Tree); *Anna Kerenina, The Rolling Stone* (Royal Exchange/West Yorkshire Playhouse); *The Railway Children* (King's Cross Station); *Pests* (Clean Break/Royal Court); *Antigone* (Pilot Theatre); *A Harlem Dream* (Young Vic/Dance Umbrella); *Billy the Girl* (Clean Break/Soho); *Hopelessly Devoted* (Paines Plough) and *Silly Kings* (National Theatre Wales). Joanna designed the 'Capturing the Flame' ceremony for the inaugural European Games in Baku, Azerbaijan. Joanna forms part of the multi-award-winning theatre company Look Left Look Right as Associate Designer.

Lee Curran (Lighting Designer)

Lee's theatre credits include *X, Linda, Constellations* (Royal Court); *Doctor Faustus, Love's Sacrifice, Arden of Faversham* (Royal Shakespeare Company); *The Spoils* (ATG/The New Group); *Splendour* (Donmar Warehouse); *The Oresteia* (Home, Manchester); *Hamlet, Much Ado About Nothing, Blindsided* (Royal Exchange, Manchester); *A Number* (Nuffield/Young Vic); *Mametz* (National Theatre of Wales); *Protest Song* (National Theatre Shed); *Depart, Turfed, 66 Minutes in Damascus* (LIFT); *Regeneration, Dancing at Lughnasa* (Northampton); *Blam!* (Neander); *The Sacred Flame* (ETT/Rose Kingston); *The Fat Girl Gets a Haircut and Other Stories, Puffball* (Roundhouse); *Clytemnestra* (Sherman Cymru); *The Rise and Shine of Comrade Fiasco, Unbroken* (Gate) and *The Empty Quarter* (Hampstead Downstairs). Dance credits include *Sun, Political Mother, The Art of Not Looking Back, In Your Rooms, Uprising* with Hofesh Shechter; *Clowns* (Nederlands Dans Theater); *Untouchable* (Royal Ballet); *Tomorrow, Frames, Curious Conscience* (Rambert Dance Company); *The Measures Taken, All That is Solid Melts into Air, The Grit in The Oyster* (Alexander Whitley); *Bastard Amber, Interloper* (Liz Roche); *There We Have Been* (James Cousins); *Wide Awakening* (Joss Arnott) and works for Rafael Bonachela, Jonzi D, and Candoco. Opera credits include *Orpheé et Eurydice* (Royal Opera House); *Ottone, Life on the Moon* (English Touring Opera) and *Nabucco* (Opera National de Lorraine).

Emma Laxton (Sound Designer)

Emma's theatre credits include *Observe the Sons of Ulster Marching Towards the Somme* (Headlong/tour); *Great Expectations* (West Yorkshire Playhouse); *Elizabeth* (Royal Opera House); *The Lion, The Witch, and the Wardrobe* (Birmingham Rep); *The Oresteia* (HOME Theatre, Manchester); *Wuthering Heights, The Merchant of Venice, Consensual* (NYT); *The Effect* (Sheffield Theatres); *Henry the Fifth* (Unicorn, Imaginate Festival); *All My Sons* (Talawa Theatre, UK tour); *Hello/Goodbye, The Blackest Black, #Aiww: The Arrest of Ai Wei Wei, Lay Down Your Cross, Blue Heart Afternoon* (Hampstead); *Accolade*

(St James); *Cat On A Hot Tin Roof* (Royal Exchange/Royal & Derngate/ Northern Stage); *The Colby Sisters of Pittsburgh, Pennsylvania* (Tricycle); *Pests* (Clean Break/Royal Exchange/Royal Court); *Coriolanus, Berenice, The Physicists, Making Noise Quietly, The Recruiting Officer* (Donmar Warehouse); *All My Sons, A Doll's House, Three Birds, The Accrington Pals, Lady Windermere's Fan* (Royal Exchange, Manchester); *Much Ado About Nothing* (Old Vic) and *nut* (National Theatre).

Emma was the Associate Sound Designer for the National Theatre's production of *War Horse*, and was previously Deputy Head of Sound for the Royal Court. Emma won the Falstaff Award for Best Sound Design/Original Score for her work on *Coriolanus* at the Donmar Warehouse in 2014.

James Fortune (Musical Director)

James's theatre credits include *The Two Gentlemen of Verona* (Shakespeare's Globe/UK tour); *The Odyssey Missing Presumed Dead* (ETT/Liverpool Everyman & Playhouse/UK tour); *Shibboleth* (Abbey, Dublin); *The Rolling Stone* (Royal Exchange/West Yorkshire Playhouse); *A Midsummer Night's Dream* (Liverpool Everyman & Playhouse); *Teh Internet is Serious Business, In the Republic of Happiness* (Royal Court); *Posh* (Royal Court/West End); *The Beautiful Cosmos of Ivor Cutler* (Vanishing Point/National Theatre of Scotland Scottish tour/Brighton Festival); *Dick Whittington and His Cat, Jack and the Beanstalk, Secret Theatre Show 1* (Lyric Hammersmith); *Our Big Land* (Romany Theatre Company) and *Coffee* (Pleasance, Edinburgh). James is currently working on the boxing musical *Journeyman* and developing *Lord of the Darts*, the second piece in his sporting musical trilogy.

As a singer and flautist he has worked with, amongst others, Tom Jones, Kate Nash and Blondie. James is also a founder member of, and arranger for, award-winning vocal harmony band The Magnets, who have appeared on *The Review Show, Comic Relief, Parkinson, GMTV, BBC Proms in the Park* and *Blue Peter* as well as sessions for Radio 1 and 2.

Sarah Dowling (Movement Director)

Sarah Dowling is a movement director, choreographer and performer. Movement direction includes *Great Expectations* (dir. by Lucy Bailey); *Waiting for Godot* (Haymarket Theatre Royal); *Julius Caeser* (RSC) and Purcell's *Fairy Queen* (Middle Temple Hall). Sarah is also currently coaching on two Warner Bros films directed David Yates: *Tarzan and Fantastic Beasts and Where to Find Them*. As a choreographer Sarah has her own company and has been an associate artist at the Royal Opera House Covent Garden and a Place Prize semi-finalist. As a performer she has worked for the past twelve years with immersive theatre specialists Punchdrunk. This is Sarah's third production in collaboration with Amy Hodge, having previously worked on *7-75*, an intergenerational piece commissioned by The Place, and *Our Big Land* (Romany Theatre Company).

Bush Theatre

We make theatre for London. Now.

The Bush is a world-famous home for new plays and an internationally renowned champion of playwrights. We discover, nurture and produce the best new writers from the widest range of backgrounds from our home in a distinctive corner of west London.

The Bush has won over 100 awards and developed an enviable reputation for touring its acclaimed productions nationally and internationally.

We are excited by exceptional new voices, stories and perspectives – particularly those with contemporary bite which reflect the vibrancy of British culture now.

Usually housed in the old Shepherd's Bush library, 2016 sees the Bush Theatre take to the streets while we transform our home into an accessible and sustainable theatre for the future.

Read more about our plans **bushtheatre.co.uk/our-plans**
Be part of our story **bushtheatre.co.uk/support**
Follow the story online **#BushBreaksOut**

Bush Theatre

Artistic Director	**Madani Younis**
Executive Director	**Jon Gilchrist**
Assistant Producer	**Lise Bell**
Community Producer	**Amanda Castro**
Head of Marketing	**Lauren Clancy**
Press Representative	**Corner Shop PR**
Literary Administrator	**Amy Davies Dolamore**
Associate Dramaturg	**Rob Drummer**
Associate Director	**Omar Elerian**
Development Officer	**Elaine Ellis**
General Manager	**Cat Gray**
Box Office Supervisor	**Farrar Hornby**
Theatre Administrator	**Anna Jones**
Head of Finance	**Candida Ronald**
Digital Content Producer	**Leonie Sheridan**
Development Officer (Trusts)	**Ine Van Riet**
Development Director	**Anna Vaughan**
Producer	**Sophie Watson**

Apprentices, Interns and Fellows
Ellie Horne

Board of Trustees
Simon Johnson (Chair), Gianni Alen-Buckley, Matthew Byam Shaw, Grace Chan, Mark Dakin, Simon Dowson-Collins, Nike Jonah, Stephen Greenhalgh, Khafi Kareem, Isabella Macpherson, Nick Starr, Madani Younis

Bush Theatre, 7 Uxbridge Road, London W12 8LJ
Box Office: 020 8743 5050 | Administration: 020 8743 3584
Email: info@bushtheatre.co.uk
bushtheatre.co.uk

The Alternative Theatre Company Ltd (The Bush Theatre) is a Registered Charity and a company limited by guarantee.
Registered in England no. 1221968
Charity no. 270080

THANK YOU
TO OUR SUPPORTERS

The Bush Theatre would like to extend a very special thank you to the following Star Supporters, Corporate Members and Trusts & Foundations whose valuable contributions help us to nurture, develop and present some of the brightest new literary stars and theatre artists.

LONE STAR
Eric Abraham
Gianni Alen-Buckley
Michael Alen-Buckley
Rafael & Anne-Helene
  Biosse Duplan
Garvin & Steffanie Brown
Siri & Rob Cope
Aditya Mittal
Miles Morland

HANDFUL OF STARS
Anonymous
Dawn & Gary Baker
Martin Bartle
Charlie Bigham
Clive and Helena Butler
Clare & Chris Clark
Clyde Cooper
Alice Findlay
Zarina Funk
Richard and Jane Gordon
Lesley Hill & Russ Shaw
Simon & Katherine Johnson
Emmie Jones
V & F Lukey
Vera Monotti Graziadei
Paige Nelson
Georgia Oetker
Philip & Biddy Percival
Robert Rooney
Joana & Henrik Schliemann
Philippa Seal & Philip Jones QC
The van Tulleken Family
Charlotte & Simon Warshaw

RISING STARS
ACT IV
Nicholas Alt
Anonymous
Melanie Aram
Tessa Bamford
Christopher Bevan
David Brooks
Maggie Burrows
Simon Burstein
Matthew Byam Shaw
Jennifer Caruso Viall
Benedetta Cassinelli
Tim & Andrea Clark
Sarah Clarke
Claude & Susie Cochin de Billy
Lois Cox
Susie Cuff
Matthew Cushen
Liz & Simon Dingemans
Andrew & Amanda Duncan
Catherine Faulks

Natalie Fellowes
Lady Antonia Fraser
Jack Gordon & Kate Lacy
Hugh & Sarah Grootenhuis
Thea Guest
Mary Harvey
Madeleine Hodgkin
Bea Hollond
Caroline Howlett
Ann & Ravi Joseph
Davina & Malcolm Judelson
Nicola Kerr
Sue Knox
Isabella Macpherson
Penny Marland
Liz & Luke Mayhew
Michael McCoy
Fiona McDougall
Judith Mellor
Caro Millington
Mark & Anne Paterson
Lauren Prakke
Barbara Prideaux
Emily Reeve
Renske & Marion Mann
Sarah Richards
Susie Saville Sneath
John & Tita Shakeshaft
Saleem & Alexandra Siddiqi
Brian Smith
Nick Starr
Peter Tausig
Marina Vaizey
Francois & Arrelle von Hurter
Trish Wadley
Amanda Waggott
Sir Robert & Lady Wilson
Peter Wilson-Smith & Kat Callo
Alison Winter

CORPORATE MEMBERS
Leading Light
Winton Capital Management
Lightbulb
The Agency (London) Ltd

PUBLIC FUNDING

Supported by
ARTS COUNCIL ENGLAND

h&f
hammersmith & fulham

SPONSORS & SUPPORTERS
Drama Centre London
Kudos Film & TV
MAC Cosmetics Markson Pianos
Nick Hern Books

The Groucho Club
The Law Society
Simon Gray Award
Waitrose Community Matters
West 12 Shopping & Leisure
  Centre
Phillip Wooller

TRUSTS AND FOUNDATIONS
The Andrew Lloyd Webber
  Foundation
The Bruce Wake Charitable Trust
The City Bridge Trust
Cockayne – Grants for the Arts
The Daisy Trust
The D'Oyly Carte Charitable Trust
EC&O Venues Charitable Trust
The Equity Charitable Trust
Eranda Rothschild Foundation
Esmée Fairbairn Foundation
Fidelio Charitable Trust
Foyle Foundation
Garfield Weston Foundation
Garrick Charitable Trust
The Gatsby Charitable Foundation
The Goldsmiths' Company
The Harold Hyam Wingate
  Foundation
Hammersmith United Charities
Heritage of London Trust
The Idlewild Trust
John Lyon's Charity
The J Paul Getty Jnr Charitable
  Trust
The John S Cohen Foundation
The John Thaw Foundation
Land Securities
The Leche Trust
The Leverhulme Trust
The London Community
  Foundation
The Martin Bowley Charitable
  Trust
The Monument Trust
Paul Hamlyn Foundation
Pilgrim Trust
The Theatres Trust
The Thistle Trust
Viridor Credits
The Williams Charitable Trust
Western Riverside Environmental
  Fund
The Wolfson Foundation
The Worshipful Company
  of Grocers

Headlong

Headlong: /hedl'ong/noun
1. with head first,
2. starting boldly,
3. to approach with speed and vigour

Headlong creates exhilarating contemporary theatre: a provocative mix of innovative new writing, reimagined classics and influential twentieth century plays that illuminate our world. Touring exceptional theatre around the UK lies at the heart of what we do; we also present work on major London stages and internationally. We encourage the best emerging artists and more established talent to do their most exciting work with us. We place digital innovation at the forefront of all our activities - building inventive online content to sit alongside our productions to enrich audiences' understanding of our work.

Our productions have included *People, Places and Things* (National Theatre and West End), *1984* (UK and international tour and West End), *The Nether* (Royal Court and West End), *Chimerica* (Almeida and West End), *American Psycho* (Almeida and Broadway) and *Enron* (UK tour, West End and Broadway).

In addition to *Boys Will Be Boys*, in 2016 Frank McGuinness' iconic WW1 play *Observe the Sons of Ulster Marching Towards the Somme* will tour the UK and Ireland from May - October directed by Headlong's

Artistic Director Jeremy Herrin. In the West End, George Orwell's canonical work *1984*, adapted by Olivier Award-winner Robert Icke and Olivier Award-nominee Duncan Macmillan will return to London's Playhouse Theatre following a sell-out international tour. Jeremy Herrin will also direct James Graham's critically acclaimed political drama *This House* which will transfer to the West End in November following its upcoming run at Chichester's Minerva Theatre.

Headlong has won numerous Olivier awards, most recently for our co-production with the National Theatre *People, Places and Things* (Best Actress Denise Gough, Best Sound Design Tom Gibbons).

> '*Slams down with that characteristic Headlong rush*'
> The Observer on *People, Places and Things*.

> '*The indefatigably inventive Headlong*'
> The Times on *1984*

> '*A touring company of generous unpredictability*'
> The Observer

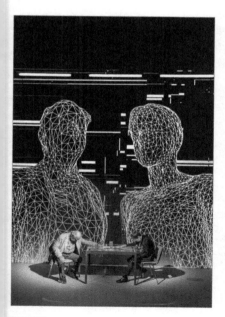

The Nether
Photo: Johan Persson

Headlong Staff

Artistic Director
Jeremy Herrin

Interim Executive Director
Fran du Pille

Finance Manager
Julie Renwick

Associate Producer
Liz Eddy

Associate General Manager
Amy Michaels

Producing Assistant
Alecia Marshall

Administrator
Ellie Claughton

Creative Associate
Amy Hodge

Associate Artist
Sarah Grochala

Production Manager
Cath Bates

Marketing Consultant
Victoria Wilson

Press Agent
Clióna Roberts

Fundraising Consultant
Kirstin Peltonen

Visit our website
www.headlong.co.uk
for news of forthcoming projects,
to join our mailing list, and to find out
how you can support our work.
Follow @HeadlongTheatre on Twitter.

BOYS WILL BE BOYS

Melissa Bubnic

Characters

ASTRID WENTWORTH, *forty-two, a Foreign Exchange broker at Peterson Jones & Walker*
PRIYA SENGUPTA, *twenty-two, her junior*
HARRISON STEVENSON, *twenty-three, also a junior*
ARTHUR BEALE, *late fifties, a senior manager*
ISABELLE, *late thirties, a prostitute*

This play is to be performed by at least five actors – all of whom are female.

All other characters named in the text are to be shared by the ensemble.

A line with no full stop at the end of a speech indicates that the next speech follows on immediately.

The use of '/' marks the point that the next line should begin.

This text went to press before the end of rehearsals and so may differ slightly from the play as performed.

One

A dimly lit cabaret club.

Punters sit at tables, talking among themselves, generally ignoring the stage.

ASTRID *sings the first verse of Peggy Lee's 'I Love Being Here with You'.*

ASTRID. How about a spotlight for the diva sweating her guts out on the floor tonight? I've been in S&M dungeons that are better lit, am I right? Am I right?

ASTRID *gets her spotlight.*

I can crawl my way up an anus by instinct alone but I need at least a lamp to find a microphone.

She sings the next three verses.

So I find myself in a bar last night... alone, I know, right? Tits like these and I'm drinking alone? Am I taking crazy pills or what? So I order myself a martini, Hendricks, hundred-to-one gin-to-vermouth ratio, I like 'em dry, I'm talking Sahara dry, Gobi desert dry, I want sand in a motherfucking glass is what I want and the bartender, this kid, this muscle in a white shirt and vest, this wannabe actor, dancer whatever the fuck his dream is, he hands me my drink and says to me, 'It's on the house.'

And I'm thinking we should fuck now in the toilets and that way I won't have to wait until the end of his shift when I look into his eyes and see not desire, but pity. He feels sorry for me. This minimum-wage nobody feels sorry for *me*. *He* feels sorry for *me*. *Me*. Like I'm some fucking character in a Billy Joel song. Like I've been sitting there crying into my sumac-spiced almonds. Is that who I am now?

She sings the fifth and the sixth verses.

I find myself in a bar last night... alone (I know, it's fucking ridiculous, could've saved myself that Brazilian, it's the equivalent of storing Monet's water lilies in a broom closet, seriously) and a barman's look sends me stumbling, tits-over-arse backwards into memory lane, to playground tan bark and the metallic smell of monkey bars and bloody shredded knees and the last time I saw pity... So I'm five, right? And my best friend in the world is James Kokkinos and he's sorry, he's really sorry, but we can't be friends any more, we can't colour in Garfield comics or play King of the Mountain because he's with the boys now, he's in boys' world and I can't come with because, y'know, I'm not packing the necessary equipment.

She sings the final verse.

So I find myself in a bar last night... alone and realise that I knew it when I was five, that the real difference between men and women was not wee-wees or pee-pees, but the worlds they get to live in. There's boys' world and there's girls' world and I've never been one for plaiting hair and playing house but how do you get into boys' world when you've got a vagina?

Two

Peterson Jones & Walker office.

ASTRID *is interviewing* PRIYA SENGUPTA.

ASTRID. What drives you?

PRIYA. Money.

ASTRID. And why do you want to be an FX broker?

PRIYA. To make a lot of money.

ASTRID. Brokers don't make money. We're flies on the dung heap – and it's not even our dung – we just sift some particles off the top.

PRIYA. The good brokers make money. And I will be a good broker.

ASTRID. Who, living or dead, would you most like to meet and why?

PRIYA. Warren Buffett so I can get investment tips. So I can make a lot of money.

ASTRID. What are your outside interests?

PRIYA. Why would I have those? All I want to do is make a lot of money.

ASTRID. And what –

PRIYA. The answer is money – to make a lot of money.

ASTRID. You've come across a man on a bridge. He's going to commit suicide because he's lost everything. Which of the following three things do you say? A: There's a lot of people who care about you. B: I can find you a new job. C: Go ahead and jump.

PRIYA. Helping others takes time. Time I could use to make money for my company and myself. Screw the losers and move on. C: Go ahead and jump.

ASTRID. You'd really tell a suicidal man to jump? Really? Or you think I'm that big a cunt that's what I want to hear?

Beat.

PRIYA. No, I'm sorry, no.

ASTRID. Would you tell a suicidal man to jump?

PRIYA. No, I wouldn't. I wouldn't stop to speak to him at all.

ASTRID. What specifically excites you about currency trading?

PRIYA. You.

PRIYA *has* ASTRID*'s attention.*

You have the most impressive client list at the best brokerage in the City.

ASTRID. I don't have Morgan Stanley.

PRIYA. Not yet.

ASTRID. Honey, if you're looking for a woman to mentor you, I'm no friend to the sisterhood. I'm basically a man who sits to pee.

PRIYA. I don't want a woman, I want the best.

ASTRID. How do you think this interview is going?

PRIYA. I think you like me.

ASTRID. Is it important to you to be liked?

PRIYA *falters for the first time*.

Take this job and people, I mean outsiders, will hate you. They think we caused the crash, we took away people's homes, it's our fault they can't buy a house, or can't sell it or whatever. They think you've made a pact with the devil. They want you to be that lonely career woman, they need you to be that lonely career woman. Nothing in the fridge but a bottle of Dom and expired milk. That's the narrative, right? Brokers are evil, because we sold our souls.

PRIYA. What do you say? When someone tells you you've sold your soul?

ASTRID. I say it's mine to sell. And the devil knows how to dance. Why be a broker, really? And don't tell me money cos I don't believe you.

PRIYA. I'm not supposed to be here. That's the thing – I'm not supposed to be here. I'm supposed to be an accountant. I'm supposed to work in IT. I'm supposed to be good with numbers and codes and do what Asian girls do – be competent but not in a way that's threatening. I'm supposed to be successful but not want to be successful, not too much. Everything is just... don't get greedy, don't want too much. But I do want. I want everything. I want to win. I'm here to win.

ASTRID. Your whole 'I'm all about the money' thing, it's cute – you're right, I actually do kind of like you. So take this in the spirit in which it's meant – don't be a broker.

PRIYA. What?

ASTRID. You should work in equities or pensions. You should work in a bank, in a nice office, with nice people, and have a nice life.

PRIYA. I'm sorry?

ASTRID. Good luck... (*Checks the name.*) Priya Sengupta.

PRIYA. I don't understand, I have a first from MIT, I aced the first three rounds of interviews, is it something I said?

ASTRID. Sweetheart, take it as a compliment. I told you, brokers, we're flies on shit, we're fucking algae, we're mouth-breathers, we're the untouchables of the City. We should all be desexed.

PRIYA. What are your concerns? I know I can convince you, I –

ASTRID. Honey, this is trench fucking warfare, okay? Your studied attempts at being a hardarse? I see through you. You're a nice fucking girl and I've got no time for nice girls.

PRIYA. Why do you think I'm nice? Cos I'm Asian? I'm not quiet and demure and off to marry my cousin in Bangladesh, okay?

ASTRID. You've been here all of ten minutes and already you're playing the race card. That shit won't fly.

PRIYA. I'm not playing any cards I –

ASTRID. There are brokers out there from China, Japan, Kuwait, Nigeria – and they're called sand monkeys, niggers, rice-eating yellow cunts. And that's just fun office banter. How will you feel when they call you poppadom, curry, when they're making innuendo about the taste of your chutney?

PRIYA. I'm tougher than I look.

ASTRID. This job is wading up to your tits in shit the entire time. You haven't seen desperation until you've seen a broker on a bad streak, day after sweaty day, pestering clients like crabs on a vulva. My first day my head threw his fucking latte in my face, a hot fucking coffee, because it was the wrong shade of brown. These are hard fucking men, each arsehole going for broke in the Arsehole Olympics. Someone gets sacked at least once a week. And there's no collection for cake and a card – they're gone like they never existed. You won't last and you know why? Because it's a shit job, for shit pay, working with shitheads.

PRIYA *has been dismissed. She gets up to leave but turns back to* ASTRID.

PRIYA. Why are you a broker? If it's shit and full of arseholes and you make no money, why do you do it?

Beat.

I'm not a nice girl. I'm like you, I'm the same as you. I want this because it's hard, because no one thinks I can do it. Please don't underestimate my gratitude in giving me this chance. I will be invaluable to you.

ASTRID. You're hungry, I'll give you that.

PRIYA. I'm ravenous.

Beat.

ASTRID. Alright, Priya Sengupta, impress me. Welcome to the City.

Three

A hotel bar.

ASTRID WENTWORTH *is drinking her third martini.*

ISABELLE *sits near her but not next to her, drinking a white wine.*

ASTRID. Don't you find it's impossible to drink alone at a hotel bar without looking like a prostitute?

ISABELLE. I am a prostitute.

ASTRID. So you see my point.

Beat.

You're really a prostitute?

ISABELLE *doesn't answer.*

Are you working right now?

ISABELLE. Are you paying me? Then no.

ASTRID. I'll give you a hundred.

ISABELLE. For what?

ASTRID. To sit next to me. So I don't look like a prostitute waiting for clients at a hotel bar.

ISABELLE. You don't think sitting with a prostitute implicates you as a prostitute?

ASTRID. No, it implicates me as a john.

ISABELLE. You're the john? I couldn't be the john?

ASTRID. Honey, please.

ISABELLE. You want me to laugh at your jokes, listen to your tales of woe, that kind of thing?

ASTRID. That kind of thing.

ISABELLE. I don't do incest stories.

ASTRID. What?

ISABELLE. Don't tell me what your daddy did. I don't care.

ASTRID. He didn't do –

ISABELLE. Or your uncle. Or that PE teacher everyone thought was such a nice guy until decades' worth of kids say how he made them put it in their mouth and threatened to kill their families if they told anyone.

ASTRID. There's no child abuse.

ISABELLE. Because I have fucking had it with child-abuse stories, okay?

ASTRID. My dad died before he could interfere with me.

ISABELLE. And there's no uncle?

ASTRID. My PE teacher was a disabled woman, used a wheelchair. Had no hands. Just… stumps.

ISABELLE. You do know the whole tart-with-a-heart stereotype is bullshit, right? I don't care about you, I'm not going to change your life, I'm not dispensing any homespun wisdom, streetwise insight, I'm not sassy, I fucking refuse to be sassy.

ASTRID. You're not Julia Roberts, I'm not Richard Gere, this is not *Pretty Woman*, understood.

ISABELLE. So what is your thing?

ASTRID. You interrogate all prospective clients with this much warmth? You have a problem working for a woman?

ISABELLE. Women are just men with less money.

Beat.

Four hundred. And I'll be your friend for an hour.

ASTRID. That's rather a lot, isn't it? For listening? At that price, I may as well cum in your face and bore you with how my disabled teacher fucked me with her stumps.

ISABELLE. I know what I'm worth.

ASTRID. Which is?

ISABELLE. As much as you'll pay.

ASTRID and ISABELLE stare at each other.

ASTRID indicates for another round…

ASTRID extends her hand for ISABELLE to shake.

ASTRID. Astrid Wentworth.

ISABELLE ignores it.

ASTRID realises, takes the money from her handbag and slides it to ISABELLE.

ISABELLE discreetly and quickly pockets it.

ISABELLE extends her hand for ASTRID to shake.

ISABELLE. Isabelle.

The two women shake hands.

ASTRID. Tell me about yourself.

ISABELLE. No.

ASTRID. Who's paying who here?

ISABELLE. You don't want to know about me. Not really.
You're just looking for a jumping-off point to talk about you.

ASTRID. How come you're so confident? Haven't you been...
y'know, beaten down by life? Don't you come from a broken
home? Weren't you gang-raped by the football team or
something and that explains... y'know.

ISABELLE. You like my confidence. It turns you on.

ASTRID. I'm not a lesbian.

ISABELLE. I didn't say you were. Gay, straight – why do we
have to operate in binary anyway?

ASTRID. I'm serious. I want to know about you. I want to
know why you say things like 'operate in binary'. I'm
paying you and I want what I want.

ISABELLE. What you want is to be intrigued. And I'm giving
you that. In spades. So you've got a room?

ASTRID. Why would I have a room?

ISABELLE. Clock's ticking.

   ASTRID *downs her martini and the two leave.*

Four

Peterson Jones & Walker office.

Ladies' bathroom.

ASTRID *is doing her hair and make-up.*

PRIYA *reads from and takes notes...*

ASTRID....so think of yourself as a grocer at a fruit market,
and you sell oranges. And punters come past all the time and
they'll ask how much for a hundred oranges, fifty, sixty, and
you'll give them a price –

*

The door opens a crack and an embarrassed HARRISON *sticks his head in.*

Outside, we hear the noise and chaos of the floor.

SPEAKER (*off stage*). How you left at the one-month?

BOOKIE 1. How we left at the one-month?

BOOKIE 2. Fifty fifty-four

BOOKIE 1 (*to* SPEAKER). Fifty fifty-four

SPEAKER. One hundred mine at fifty-four!

BOOKIE 1. Mine! Mine at fifty-four one hundred!

BOOKIE 2. Yours at fifty-four one hundred!

BOOKIE 1 (*to* SPEAKER). Yours at fifty-four!

SPEAKER. Done at fifty-four!

BOOKIE 1. Done.

SPEAKER. How you left at twenty-eight days?

ASTRID. This is Ralph. He's my other junior.

HARRISON, *still awkward about being in the ladies' room, and* PRIYA *shake hands.*

HARRISON. Harrison Stevenson.

PRIYA. Harrison? Not Ralph?

ASTRID. Everyone calls him Ralph.

HARRISON. Ralph Lauren? The implication is that I wear polo shirts and I'm a, y'know, dick.

HARRISON *smiles helplessly.*

(*To* ASTRID.) I know it has to be Heston, and I've tried to get you a table tonight but they can only do six thirty and I wasn't sure –

ASTRID. I said 9 p.m.

HARRISON. Yes, I know, and I've mentioned your name –

ASTRID. Suck off the maître d', give him your kidney, I don't give a fuck.

*

HARRISON *exits*.

BOOKIES (*off stage*). RALPH!

ASTRID (*as though they were never interrupted*). – and if they're happy with that price, you sell, and you've made a deal. And you're trying to make deals with dozens of punters at the same time.

The door swings open and HARRISON *again sticks only his head in, and we hear the chaos of the floor.*

BOOKIE 1 (*off stage*). Yours you fuckin' cunt yours!

BOOKIE 2. Mine seventy-two hundred!

BOOKIE 3. Choppy out there, boys, fuckin' choppy!

A torrent of objects are hurled at HARRISON – *he ducks*.

BOOKIES. RALPH!

PRIYA *watches horrified;* ASTRID *doesn't notice*.

HARRISON. He said he could do a late sitting at ten, if that would work…

ASTRID *gives* HARRISON *a death stare*.

But it probably wouldn't, would it? Okay, I'll um… so nine o'clock. A table for six at nine o'clock, I'll… organise… that then.

HARRISON *takes a deep breath and exits*.

The door swings closed.

BOOKIES (*off stage*). RALPH!

ASTRID (*as though they hadn't been interrupted*). But now the market moves, there's a drought in Brazil and the world's orange supply halves. So your oranges are suddenly worth a lot more. Or the opposite happens, and California and Florida have a bumper crop year and you're drowning in fucking oranges you can't give away. And those dozen punters in front of you? Now there's sixty, all of them screaming, wanting you to act now now now. An unexpected election result in Britain, a terrorist attack in China, poor employment numbers in the US – this can affect the price of cable – that's sterling and the dollar – and what looked like a bad price suddenly becomes a good price, or what looked like a good price is now a piece of shit.

ARTHUR BEALE *enters, doesn't acknowledge the women, unzips his trousers and pisses in the loo, cubicle door open.*

PRIYA *is agog.*

He whistles, finishes, washes his hands next to ASTRID.

ARTHUR. Miss Wentworth.

ASTRID. Arthur.

PRIYA *extends her hand for* ARTHUR *to shake. He's confused by the gesture ('Who is this girl?'), ignores it, and wipes his hands.*

PRIYA. Mr Beale, I'm Priya Sengupta and I wanted to say how excited I am to be working in your team at PJW. This is a dream come true, really. And you should know that your faith, Astrid's faith in me has not been –

ARTHUR *has left.*

– misplaced.

ASTRID. Arthur Beale is the only man I let use the women's toilets. You don't make the head of shop walk up a floor every time he wants to piss. He won't acknowledge you exist because you don't exist. Understand you are a gimp. If I say, 'Gimp, a four-shot skim-milk latte,' you will, gimp, get me a four-shot skim-milk latte.

ASTRID *throws the door open and makes* PRIYA *look out.*

Look around. Maybe one person here will still be working in five years' time. Make sure it's you. So many piggies come to market with dreams of making a killing and end up the ham. Don't become the ham. Questions?

PRIYA. When do I start my training?

ASTRID. That was your training.

Beat.

PRIYA. Yes, of course, but I mean… when do I start training how to actually… y'know, buy and sell currency? I was reading Barclays analysis on the yen and I thought –

ASTRID. No one cares what you think. I'm not impressed by regurgitation of the *Financial* fucking *Times*.

PRIYA *looks a little crestfallen.*

My first eighteen months I did nothing but coffee orders and admin. But I learned everything there is to know about the business. Keep your eyes and ears open and when I need you to be ready, you'll be ready, okay?

PRIYA *nods.*

ASTRID *winks.*

HARRISON *pops his head back in, incredibly excited.*

HARRISON. I did it! A table for six at nine o'clock at Heston!

Someone hurls a cricket ball at his face.

HARRISON *collapses on the other side of the door.*

ASTRID (*to* PRIYA). Now, gimp, get me my fucking coffee.

Five

ASTRID*'s home.*

ASTRID *is in bed.*

ISABELLE *enters, undresses, ready for bed.*

ASTRID. There's only three gong bao prawns left. There would've been more if you'd got here sooner.

ISABELLE. Sichuan again? That's what, the fourth time this week?

ASTRID. If I wanted someone to break my balls I'd be married. Where've you been?

ISABELLE. Negotiating a peace agreement between Palestine and Israel. We failed but the hummus was excellent.

ASTRID. Tell me about him.

ISABELLE. You know where I'd be without discretion? Ripped stockings in broken heels blowing lorry drivers at the back of service stations.

ASTRID. Tell me.

ISABELLE. It's a question of ethics, the code of confidentiality between client and service provider is sacrosanct. How can my clients trust me with their erectile dysfunction, their disappointed fathers, their wives' depression, their children's learning difficulties, their own debts and fears and insecurities and panic – if I don't keep their secrets?

ASTRID. You never give me what I want.

ISABELLE. My soul is mine to keep. You get everything else, babe.

ASTRID. I want all of you. Soul included. Or what differentiates me from all the other City pricks?

Beat.

ISABELLE. He's thirty-five, thirty-six. Real-estate financing, in-house for JP Morgan. Hugo Boss charcoal-grey slim-fit wool suit, white-gold cufflinks engraved RAB he got as a gift, maybe from his parents, or grandmother on graduating from university –

ASTRID. He's sentimental.

ISABELLE. Real family man. His wife picks out his ties. She's got better taste than him and he defers to her opinion. Today it's metallic grey.

ASTRID. What does the wife do?

ISABELLE. HR in a regional hospital. They moved out of the city so they could afford a nice four-bedroom house, in a nice town, somewhere you throw your chicken bones in the bin – he didn't want to leave but she was tired of her commute, and this way she's closer to her mum who babysits the kids during the day.

ASTRID. Kids? Plural?

ISABELLE. Two, definitely. She'd like a third but he's resistant. She miscarried earlier this year and he hates himself for it, but he was relieved when she came out of the bathroom with blood on her hands, crying.

ASTRID. And what did he want from you?

ISABELLE. To fuck. In the most pedestrian way possible.

Beat.

Sated? Now you know you're the most interesting person in my life?

ASTRID. Bet you say that to all the boys.

ISABELLE. I do, but with you I really mean it.

ASTRID. Do you hate them? Men?

ISABELLE. They're not men, they're clients. And no, I don't hate men.

ASTRID. You must, a little.

ISABELLE. Why would you say that?

ASTRID. I just assumed when you have someone's sweaty balls in your face you might feel a bit revolted.

ISABELLE. As opposed to your delicate muff flower? Work is work. Some tasks are more unpleasant than others. I've always got along well with men. Much more so than women.

ASTRID. That's because you're beautiful. Attractive women always get along well with men, and never with other women.

ISABELLE. I get along well with you.

ASTRID. I'm not like other women.

ISABELLE. There was a man who ran the bakery. Mr Pierce, the baker. You'd think a baker would be more jolly, fat and happy eating cakes. But he was thin and miserable. I was eight. It was hot. I was wearing these little shorts and a pink tank top, and I saw him staring at my legs. And when I caught him staring he was embarrassed and looked away. And I was so pleased.

ASTRID. I have great legs, great tits, a fantastic smile. Men want to fuck me. They always have. My friends, my mentors, my advocates have always been men. I've never been that kind of 'let's sit around and talk about why he didn't call' kind of woman, y'know?

ISABELLE. Hm-hm.

ASTRID. You're the first female friend I've ever had.

ISABELLE. You think we're friends?

ASTRID. Friendly.

ISABELLE. You're getting all *Fried Green Tomatoes* on me. Should we adopt a Chinese baby together? You already love Sichuan food.

ASTRID. You're not afraid I'm going to fuck your husband, or take your job, or show you up. You're not threatened by me.

ISABELLE. Careful, Astrid, you're falling in love.

ASTRID. Love? Me?

ISABELLE. I'm fond of you, but you shouldn't get attached.

ASTRID. Never.

Six

A cabaret club.

ASTRID *addresses her audience, who, again, are only half-listening.*

The instrumental for Rosemary Clooney's 'Hey There' plays as ASTRID *tells her story.*

ASTRID. You know when you're a little girl you dream a lot, don't you? You dream how your life is going to turn out. And in my little-girl dreams my life was going to turn out like an American indy film starring Diane Keaton. We'd be a middle-class family on an elm-lined street in a huge white-brick house with a driveway that you would call modest even though it can comfortably accommodate two four-wheel

drives. And you'd see my sons shooting hoops above the
garage, Bobby, Jackson and little Oscar, blue-green eyes and
sandy brown hair, really handsome, really fucking… I mean
if I wasn't their mother and twenty years younger, y'know
what I'm saying? And my daughter, Emmaline, and me have
our problems, because she's exploring her sexuality which
means she dresses like a fucking farmhand, and I'm like,
'Why can't a dyke rock a strong silhouette?' and my sons
have their problems too, of course, Bobby's knocked up a
Mexican girl, and that's awkward cos you know she's not
going to abort, and Jackson's a 'writer', but really just
smokes weed and envies others, and little Oscar never grew
out of his anxiety phase and suffers quite debilitating panic
attacks but we're a family and we love each other and we
have just the right amount of dysfunction, enough to make us
real, but not too much to spoil family celebrations and our
house looks like an interior in *Elle Decor*, we've got Scandi
chic coming out the wazu, it's so fucking white and spacious
I don't know whether I'm entering the living room or a really
large fridge. And my husband, Bert, is a successful dentist
but he starts to withdraw from me, we don't make love on
Thursday nights any more which I say is fine but privately
I'm worried and I see a plastic surgeon about the cellulite on
my thighs. So when Bert has his licence revoked for fucking
his patient, that tramp divorcee, Erica Dal Tio, to whom he
gave four grand worth of dental work for free (weak gums),
of course I'm shocked but I'm not entirely surprised. But the
kids are taking my side, which is nice, because it's obviously
Bert's midlife crisis, he loves me, but he's not in love with
me, so he moves out, I see a couple of men, to show I've
moved on, but nothing serious, cos I haven't moved on, and
I find the lump, when I'm showering with my Ortigia Orange
Blossom soap, and it's Christmas Eve, and all my babies are
home, and I'm bald and using an oxygen mask and we're
sharing a joint because we're open-minded and I am dying,
and Bert knocks on the door, and he has an exquisite bunch
of white tulips, my favourite flower, and he says, 'Is there
room for me?' and I respond (because I have mentally
rehearsed this a few times), 'You don't deserve me.' And he
knows, and he starts walking down our modest but enormous
driveway, but I throw a dove-grey cashmere blanket around

my shoulders and run out after him, I swing him around and
say a little breathless, my cheeks a little flushed, 'Lucky for
you, I've always sold myself short' because even though he's
a cunt who's devastated and publicly humiliated me, I'm the
bigger person because it's not about winning but just getting
what you want and I want Bert, at least I don't want to be
alone, and he cries and I cry and we kiss passionately, but
not open-mouth because you're not allowed to over sixty and
when I die, I have the most beautiful service, the chapel full
of white tulips and my daughter Emmaline, rocking a strong
silhouette in a beautiful black suit, sings Sarah McLachlan's
'Angel' and there's not a dry eye in the house.

ASTRID *sings Rosemary Clooney's 'Hey There'.*

Seven

A pub.

ASTRID *pops down drinks for her and* ARTHUR.

ARTHUR. Dick Stevenson phoned me this afternoon.

ASTRID. Yes?

ARTHUR. Told him his boy, his boy…?

ASTRID. Harrison.

ARTHUR. Harrison. Told him young Harrison was thriving.
A natural. Am I a liar?

ASTRID. The boy's a cunt.

ARTHUR. Fuck.

ASTRID. Poor prick has been told every day since he squirted
out of his mother's slime that he's special when he's about as
useful as wet shit. He even looks stupid. I mean, he looks
like a cow, all eyeballs.

ARTHUR. Give the boy a line.

ASTRID. Are you hallucinating? The boy's a total liability! He doesn't know his yen from his arsehole. I ordered a ham and cheese flatbread and a four-shot skim-milk latte and he came back with a tomato pesto baguette and a cappuccino. And I saw him write the fucking order down!

ARTHUR. Give him a small line then.

ASTRID. Arthur –

ARTHUR. Miss Wentworth, I'm not losing my biggest client just because his son happens to be a tit. Harrison Stevenson will not be the first bookie you've made look good.

ASTRID. You mean I do the work and he takes the credit?

ARTHUR. Just until we can get him promoted elsewhere.

ASTRID. Sengupta's good.

ARTHUR. The Indian girl?

ASTRID. She was born here and her parents are Bangladeshi.

ARTHUR *doesn't understand what* ASTRID *is talking about.*

She's not Indian.

ARTHUR *still doesn't understand.*

It's a different country, Arthur.

ARTHUR. The fuck do I care?

ASTRID. She's been here almost a year and I was going to give her a line. She's smart and she works hard. She's got a lot to learn but she's got talent.

ARTHUR. You're leading somewhere?

ASTRID. She's ready for a line.

ARTHUR *shrugs as if to ask, 'So?'*

So you've got me giving Harrison a line instead.

ARTHUR. Oh dear, Miss Wentworth, is life unfair? Heavens to Betsy, call me Roger and fuck me sideways, I'm aghast at the injustice.

ASTRID. I have a proposal for you, Arthur, how everyone can get a line, how there are more than enough lines to go around.

ARTHUR. So you reveal your motive at last. And here I thought you were buying me drinks because you enjoy our tête-à-têtes.

ASTRID. Peter Stafford.

ARTHUR. What about him?

ASTRID. I want his lines.

Beat.

ARTHUR. They're not available.

ASTRID. And if I say they are?

ARTHUR. Who've you been talking to?

ASTRID. All of Peter's clients will drop him.

ARTHUR. Morgan Stanley wouldn't –

ASTRID. Peter's contact at Morgan Stanley will be redundant by the end of this week. And I'm in with the replacement, Jacob Vibert.

ARTHUR. I don't care who you're in with – it's Peter's line.

ASTRID. Which he has fisted into the ground! His spread today on the two-month sterling was wider than the fucking continent of Europe! He's a drunk, Arthur, and a cokehead. He's hitting prices like an ADHD kid at an arcade game.

ARTHUR. Why are you gunning for Peter? You used to work for him, didn't you? Years ago at ASF when you were coming up. What did he do? Insist on a couple rounds of 'hide the salami'?

ASTRID. Really, Arthur? Dick jokes? This is what we're doing now?

ARTHUR. I'm right, aren't I? This is a personal vendetta. You want me to stab someone in the back, I wanna know why I'm holding the knife.

ASTRID. He's a shit bookie with good lines that I can work better. You know it, I know it, and Peter, if he was straight long enough to read a spreadsheet, he'd know it.

ARTHUR. How long you been working this? Wooing his
clients, poisoning everyone against him? Six months, a year?
Two years? Or your entire career?

ASTRID. The real question, Arthur, is do you really care?

ARTHUR. We came up together, Miss Wentworth. He's been
my friend some twenty years.

ASTRID. And if you want someone to big-note himself in all
the old war stories, Peter's your man. But all his clients will
pull their business.

ARTHUR. If all of this is a fait accompli, why are we meeting
here like this, like a couple of Shakespeare villains behind
the curtains?

ASTRID. Because I know you, Arthur. I know you like things
clean. And it's cleaner if you take Peter out for a drink
tomorrow, explain the situation, away from the office.

ARTHUR. Thing you're forgetting, Miss Wentworth, is I don't
want to get rid of Peter. He may be a dinosaur past his prime,
but there's a familiarity to him, he's like wallpaper that I never
much cared for but don't want to see stripped out all the same.

ASTRID. I thought you might feel that way, Arthur, so I'll cut
you in on my bro on Morgan Stanley. Twenty per cent for the
first year. Compensation for facilitating this smooth
transition. I'm a generous soul, Arthur, and I always look out
for my friends.

ISABELLE *enters, is surprised to find* ASTRID *is with*
ARTHUR.

ASTRID *waves her over.*

Speaking of friends, Arthur, have you met my good friend,
Isabelle?

ARTHUR. Good evening, Isabelle.

ISABELLE. Good evening, Arthur.

ASTRID *strokes* ISABELLE'*s hair.*

ASTRID. Arthur and I were just expounding on the importance
of friendship, how it's important to know who your friends
are, and make sure they're taken care of.

ISABELLE. I'd be only too happy to take care of Astrid's friends. Any time they want.

ARTHUR. Would you now? Would you indeed?

Eight

Peterson Jones & Walker office.

The hoot calls out prices. We see text scrolling across screens...

PRIYA *and* HARRISON *sit at their desks.*

HARRISON *has a phone receiver stuck to his ear.*

PRIYA *cold-calls clients, trying to get their business...*

PRIYA. Ivan, hi, it's Priya Sengupta, we met at – No, it's Priya. *Pri-ya*, with a P. P-R-I –

Ivan's hung up.

PRIYA *throws the phone down, frustrated.*

HARRISON *still has a phone stuck to his ear.*

Harrison, who are you talking to? You've been on that same call for hours.

HARRISON. They superglued the phone. When I answered it was Ian calling me a cunt. Every time I try to call out I can't get through, cos someone's calling in to call me a cunt. They call it cunt-bombing. It'd be quite funny if it was happening to someone else.

PRIYA. What if you told your dad? He could make a call to Arthur and –

HARRISON. You think my dad doesn't know what bookies do to juniors? He sent me here to make me... to make me.

Beat.

I only have to last until I'm twenty-five and then I get my mother's inheritance and I can do... something else.

PRIYA. Like what?

HARRISON. Why are you so interested?

PRIYA. You've been handed everything I've ever wanted and you want something else. I'm curious.

HARRISON. You wouldn't get it.

PRIYA. I'm smarter than you, I would get it.

HARRISON. It's not about 'smart', it's –

PRIYA. It's so embarrassing you can't even say it?

HARRISON. I can say it –

PRIYA. So say it.

HARRISON. I... I want to be a performer, a comedian.

Beat.

I knew you wouldn't get it.

PRIYA. I get the concept, I'm just... like telling jokes? Like standing up, with a microphone, in a room of people, and telling jokes?

HARRISON. It's not so much, old-school like that, it's more –

PRIYA. But you're not funny.

HARRISON. I am funny.

PRIYA. No, you're not. You've never made me laugh. Not intentionally.

HARRISON. It's not about 'funny', it's... observations, storytelling, it's seeing the world in a unique way –

PRIYA. A white man's point of view – that is unique.

HARRISON. I don't mean –

PRIYA. See, I'm funnier than you and I'm not even trying.

HARRISON. Stephen Fry has tweeted about me – I am funny. I was the treasurer of fucking Footlights!

(*Off* PRIYA's *blank expression.*) I'm good at it.

Beat.

See me right now, you see me? Face stuck to a phone, bruises all over my back, that incident in the lift yesterday, all of that is... when you tell it as a story, it's better than real life.

PRIYA. You're too sensitive for this place.

HARRISON. I'm Dick Stevenson's son, and this is their only chance to take down someone like me, because they worry one day they'll have to kiss my arse. And they leave you alone because you're a woman, and ethnically diverse –

PRIYA. What?

HARRISON. Stick it to the rich white boy, no one cares. But go after a protected class like you and there's a potential lawsuit to worry about.

PRIYA. You're so right. We brown girls have had it easy since the British invaded the subcontinent, apart from all the raping and pillaging.

HARRISON. Touché, I'm a prick.

PRIYA. No, just naive.

HARRISON. And cute, just a little bit cute? In a pathetic, puppy-dog –

PRIYA. Pedigree Pekingnese, embarrassed-for-having-such-stupid-hair kind of way –

HARRISON. Kind of way, yeah?

PRIYA *and* HARRISON *smile at each other.*

ASTRID *enters holding a women's suit and a pair of heels.*

ASTRID (*to* HARRISON). Congratulations, you've got a line.

HARRISON *looks more scared than excited.*

Bank Populaire. You speak French, right?

HARRISON. Oui. I mean, merci. I mean... thank you.

ASTRID. Call your dad, let him know the good news.

HARRISON *looks at the receiver stuck to his ear.*

PRIYA. Use the phone in the conference room.

HARRISON *unplugs the phone, the receiver still stuck to his ear.*

HARRISON *leaves and a stapler is hurled at him.*

BOOKIES. RALPH!

ASTRID *and* PRIYA *look at each other.*

ASTRID. What business are you in?

PRIYA. Sorry…?

ASTRID. Are you selling gym membership?

PRIYA *doesn't understand the question.*

I said, are you selling gym membership or pet insurance or a lifetime supply of high-fibre muesli?

PRIYA. You know that I'm not selling gym membership, pet insurance –

ASTRID. Then why do you look like you're working in a call centre? What are you wearing?

PRIYA. Sorry?

ASTRID *hands* PRIYA *the designer suit and Christian Louboutin heels.*

PRIYA *changes out of her off-the-rack suit and her flats for the designer apparel.*

ASTRID. You want a line? You need to look like someone who works good lines. Dior, Chanel, Prada makes you look like you make serious money. That means you make clients serious money. That means clients want to do business with you so you can make serious money for them. This isn't hard – how you look matters. I know an expensive watch from a cheap one. I can tell from a man's cufflinks what school he went to. I can tell from the cut of his suit what school he's sending his kids to. How you look matters. And do you know how you look? Like a lesbian in the fucking public sector.

PRIYA. Glynnis shops at H&M.

ASTRID. Glynnis works in statistical analysis. She can wear a fucking beard and dog shit for shoes and d'you know why? Because Glynnis doesn't exist. What do you do?

PRIYA. You mean...? I'm a broker.

ASTRID. No, you're a gimp who wants to become a broker. There's a distinction.

PRIYA. I'm a gimp who / wants to become –

ASTRID. But let's say you are a broker, what do you do?

PRIYA. I make clients money.

ASTRID. What do you do?

PRIYA. I stay on top of the market. I know what my clients want / and I –

ASTRID. What do you do?

PRIYA. I buy currency.

ASTRID. What do you do?

PRIYA. I sell currency –

ASTRID. What do you do?

PRIYA. I don't know what I do!

ASTRID. You whore.

Beat.

PRIYA. I whore? You mean... I'm selling sex without my knowledge?

ASTRID. You do whatever it takes to make clients like you. Brokers are at the bottom of the food chain. For every client there's a fucking rat's nest of bookies clamouring for his business. You want to be top rat – the client has to like you. You laugh at his jokes. You get him whatever he wants – concert tickets, sporting events, coke – whatever he wants, you make him like you.

PRIYA. I understand the importance of corporate hospitality, really / I'm trying –

ASTRID. Do you understand?

PRIYA. I can't even get them to answer the phone, never mind getting them to a club so I can laugh at their jokes and buy

them coke! I could offer those… sexist fuckers a helicopter
and a blowjob from Beyoncé but they'd never know it cos
I can't get past their fucking… 'FUCK OFF!'

ASTRID. How many woman brokers are at this firm?

PRIYA. There's you… and me, the gimp who wants to become
one.

ASTRID. And why do you think that is?

PRIYA *shrugs*.

Because most women don't want to be whores. They haven't
got the stomach for it.

PRIYA. And what, the men just love bending over?

ASTRID. The men don't realise they are bending over.

PRIYA. But we do?

ASTRID. We do, and we do it better. Always know what it is
you're selling. Look at them, the bookies out on the floor.
All cleanly shaven, identikit haircuts. They all did rugby or
rowing or hockey. They're all wearing the same grey Tom
Ford suit. A pink or yellow or green tie, a hint of colour that
says they're fun but you can still trust them. It's like looking
into an infinity mirror of tedium. So why does a client call
you and not them?

PRIYA. Because I'm better.

ASTRID. A client calls you because you're not them. A client
calls you because you are a woman. A client calls you
because you're hot and he wants to be around hot women.
Plus you're Asian, and you can bet he's got a Raj/subaltern
porn fantasy. He wants to flirt with you. He wants to fuck
you. Don't fuck them but be fuckable.

PRIYA. I'm trying to be taken seriously, as a player, as an
equal, and you want me to play Bollywood princess and
emphasise my cleavage?

ASTRID. Why d'you think you got this job? You think
I would've hired you if you were ugly?

Beat.

Men want to collect pretty things. You have to be desirable. So when the smell of Hugo Boss on another twenty-year-old boy makes him sick, it's you he calls.

PRIYA. I don't want to... I don't need to do that. I will make them money. That's a lot more useful than being a fucking bauble.

ASTRID. You think this is an even-level playing field? What are you, twelve? If that was true, where are the women?

Beat.

PRIYA. So I... whore?

ASTRID. You whore.

PRIYA. I laugh at his jokes. I get him whatever he wants – concert tickets, sporting events, coke. Whatever he wants, I make him like me.

ASTRID. We don't just dance. We do everything Fred Astaire can do, but backwards, and in heels.

PRIYA *is now dressed in her new clothes, remade in* ASTRID's *image.*

ASTRID *smiles approvingly.*

So let's whore.

Nine

A strip club.

ASTRID *and* PRIYA *entertain* TRADERS 1 *and* 2.

TRADER 1. ...and the next thing he knows, get this, he wakes up in the chalet with that fucking cunt's balls being waved in his face. He's trying to teabag him, would you fucking believe it!

ASTRID (*to waitress*). Yes, we'll have twelve more crack babies and another bottle of Dom.

TRADER 1. So then he got done for assault! How'd you like that, Priya? Imagine being teabagged by your fucking client!

ASTRID. Everyone's choking on something, may as well come with commission.

TRADER 1. He was a loose cannon you know? Killed his wife's mini Yorkie. He dropped so much K on his shoes and little Alfonse (that was the Yorkie, little Alfonse) licked it up and... y'know, he had no constitution for hard drugs, being a small dog.

TRADER 2. Didn't he kill himself?

TRADER 1. Who? The Yorkie?

TRADER 2. No, Donald.

TRADER 1. Who the fuck's Donald?

TRADER 2. Aren't we talking about Donald Richardson?

TRADER 1. Are we?

ASTRID. He did kill himself. Jumped in front of a train. Morning peak hour.

TRADER 1. Jesus.

ASTRID. Caused chaos with the District line for over an hour.

TRADER 2. Got any bugle? There's a distinct shortage. My dealer is on his way but his missus is having a shit-fit because of their kid. Autism or something.

TRADER 1 *indicates he has some and offers to* ASTRID *and* PRIYA, *who politely decline*.

TRADER 1 *disappears with* TRADER 2.

ASTRID *surveys* PRIYA, *who looks very uncomfortable*.

ASTRID. Having a good time?

PRIYA *smiles politely – but no, she isn't having a good time*.

Have a drink, for fuck's sakes. Being around these douchebags sober is like a hysterectomy without anesthetic.

PRIYA. I don't really drink this much.

ASTRID. So you keep saying. You know that can't last. People will notice and trust me, Priya, if there's one thing people who are balls-deep in vice hate, it's those who abstain. Guys

like Tweedledee and Tweedledum are too insecure to get
fucked up on their own. They feel judged.

PRIYA. I don't judge –

ASTRID. Of course you fucking do. Drink.

ASTRID gives PRIYA a shot.

PRIYA doesn't want it but drinks it anyway.

PRIYA. I don't know how you drink like this and still make it to
your desk by 7 a.m.

ASTRID. Years of practice. I'll probably be dead by fifty. Fuck it.
I'd rather be dead than old. This your first time in a strip club?

PRIYA. I'm fine.

ASTRID. Then why do you look so guilty?

PRIYA. What someone does for money is their choice – I don't
feel guilty about other people's choices.

PRIYA reluctantly drinks another shot.

ASTRID. But you do feel guilty. Because you find an arse
hanging out of a ruched G-string somehow undignified. And
therefore everyone part of it, the girls, the punters, you, is
touched by something… unseemly. And it's making your
skin crawl. Drink.

PRIYA. I never said anything was… unseemly but if it was –
and I didn't say it was but if it was –

PRIYA reluctantly downs another shot.

– I'm sure these women are well compensated for any
alleged indignity and are, y'know, probably very intelligent,
empowered, fully actualised / human beings –

ASTRID. Empowered? Empowered? And how would you
know? Their job is to make you feel like they're having
a good time getting you off so they smile, laugh at your
jokes, and squeeze their nipples with wet fingers, does that
make them empowered?

PRIYA. You're saying they're not?

ASTRID. I'm saying I don't have the first fucking clue. It's the sort of thing men would say. They tell you the strippers are empowered. This is what they want to talk about with some chick's talc-swathed buttocks rubbing against their erection. 'I love this place cos the women here are so empowered. There's nothing more beautiful than the female form.' Bullshit. No one gives a fuck if they're empowered. It's none of our business if they're empowered. I don't ask my cleaner when she's bleaching my toilet if she feels empowered. When someone's performing a service, I want them to perform the service and their own feelings about it aren't my concern.

TRADERS 1 *and* 2 *return, wiping their noses.*

TRADER 1. So he danced around a bit, then sat in a plate of sausage rolls.

TRADER 2. Normal-sized sausage rolls or miniature ones?

TRADER 1. Miniature.

TRADER 2. Nice.

PRIYA. Gentlemen, y'know I've never had a lap dance.

TRADER 1. Fuck off! Really? That's like, inhuman or a violation of something.

PRIYA *calls a* STRIPPER *over, hands her cash.*

PRIYA. It's my first time – make it special.

STRIPPER *dances for* PRIYA.

ASTRID *smiles at* PRIYA *approvingly.*

TRADER 2. This is like… (*Sniffs.*) an unprecedented nirvana, y'know… (*Sniffs.*) for those who appreciate the charm and splendour of the female… don't you just want to snort vast amounts of shovel off her tits?

ASTRID. Relax, Priya. She's empowered, you're empowered, everyone's empowered.

TRADER 1. Absofuckinglutely! If there's one thing these girls are, it's –

TRADER 2. Empowered!

Ten

A hotel room.

ARTHUR. So what'll you have to drink, Isabelle?

ISABELLE. I'm fine, thank you, Arthur.

ARTHUR. One drink.

ISABELLE. We've already had more than one drink.

ARTHUR. This is a different venue so it doesn't count.

ISABELLE. You don't have to get me drunk. I'm not here for the view.

ARTHUR *hands* ISABELLE *a drink.*

He stares her down until she drinks it.

ARTHUR. You don't like me, do you?

ISABELLE. Why would you say that?

ARTHUR. Because you're a good judge of character.

ISABELLE. You want me to dislike you? Okay. You want a scared little girl, this is my first time, I'm trying to pay my way through dental school, I can be that. You want Isabelle from Estonia, I come to this country with no English, now look, I feed whole village. You can put things inside me, like Lego – is okay. I can be that. Whatever you want.

ARTHUR. Tell me what I want.

ISABELLE *considers* ARTHUR *carefully.*

ISABELLE. You like strong women. You've got no time for princesses. For you, disdain is foreplay.

ARTHUR. So I enjoy your contempt?

ISABELLE. The more I hate you the more satisfying it is to break me, to humiliate me. It's no fun breaking something that's already broken.

ARTHUR. Assuming that was true, Isabelle, why am I bothering with you at all? You're the very definition of broken. For the change in my coat pocket you'd let me shit on you. And if you're gonna pop a squat over a girl, you at least want her to act squeamish. You've got nothing –

ISABELLE. Nothing except your interest.

ARTHUR. My interest is in why Astrid sent you my way.

ISABELLE. She wants to make you happy, obviously.

ARTHUR. I'm more curious about what's not obvious here. I know I'm being played but I can't think why. Astrid knows I make decisions based on the best outcome, and if I want my dick sucked I can buy my own whore. Unless this is about you and not me?

ARTHUR*'s assessment has had a bigger impact on* ISABELLE *than she lets on.*

ISABELLE. I'm not paid to think.

ARTHUR. Right. You're the first woman without an opinion. Y'know what I value about this business? The business I'm in, not your business –

ISABELLE. Are they so different? Screwing for profit?

ARTHUR. Everyone screws for profit in every fucking business. No, what I like about broking is the honesty, the directness. If the UN worked the same way as my team on the floor? Syria would be done in a week – and at a fraction of the cost. Take off your shoes.

ISABELLE *complies.*

ISABELLE. Directness and honesty aren't the same thing.

ARTHUR. Lie down on your stomach.

ISABELLE *lies down on her stomach.*

ARTHUR *takes off his belt, and loops it around* ISABELLE*'s neck. He tightens the 'collar' and straddles her back.*

ISABELLE. One of my clients, he liked me to call him at 11:35 every Saturday. One Saturday I call him but he doesn't answer, a woman does. I hang up. She calls back. Obviously I don't pick up. She leaves a voice message.

He's dead. He hung himself from the exposed Tudor beam in their loft conversion. That's the second one I've lost this year. The other threw himself in front of a train. Fucked up the District line for an hour.

ARTHUR. Your point?

ISABELLE. These so-called honest bankers would rather die than tell the truth about themselves.

ARTHUR. I should be lectured about honesty from a woman whose job is lying? Laughing at jokes that aren't funny, admiring cocks that aren't impressive, fucking like it's the best thing since cheesecake –

ISABELLE *flips herself out of* ARTHUR*'s hold, and faces him, which takes him totally by surprise.*

ISABELLE. What I do is help you play pretend. When you're with me, you can believe you're handsome, you're interesting, I want you. That's what you pay for – but we both know it's pretend, and that's not the same as lying. It's sex with your wife that's dishonest, cos we call it romance, love, and that's just pretend without saying so. Women hate whores because we get paid more and don't have to live with you, and men hate us cos we do the work you think we should do for free.

Beat.

ARTHUR. You're right. I will enjoy humiliating you.

ISABELLE *stares at him, then lies down on her stomach.*

ARTHUR *tightens his belt around her neck, pulling her back until she's arched and uncomfortable.*

Eleven

A restaurant.

ASTRID. That's a very expensive Wagyu rib-eye you're letting get cold.

ISABELLE. I'm not hungry.

ASTRID. So you keep saying.

ISABELLE. I didn't ask you to order it.

ASTRID. Out of courtesy to the cow who laid down its life, have a bite at least.

ISABELLE. Will you be fucking me tonight? Because if you don't mind, I think… I think I need the night off.

ASTRID. Night off sex or off me?

ISABELLE. Just… night off. If you can just tell me what it is you want –

ASTRID. I want to exchange witty banter. I want to tell you about my day and hear about yours. I don't know about sex, I hadn't thought that far ahead but I'm not particularly fussed if you'd prefer not to.

ISABELLE. I could get someone to fill in. Her name's Irene. Very smart. Almost did an MBA.

ASTRID. 'Fill in'?

ISABELLE. Do this. Be here with you, eat steak, and talk about your day.

ASTRID. I don't want someone to fill in, I want you.

ISABELLE. What is this? What am I to you?

ASTRID. Have you got your period or something?

ISABELLE. Can't you answer the question? What is this? Dinners, and sleepovers, and banter –

ASTRID. This is… You've had regular clients before.

ISABELLE. Yes, and they were clients and I was the service provider. I was about as involved in their lives as the person who cleans their pool. The boundaries were clear. These boundaries are not clear.

ASTRID. I don't know what you're talking about.

ISABELLE. This right now. This is not fucking. This is… your stab at intimacy. Next, you'll ask me to meet your parents.

ASTRID. And if I did, so what? Aren't you well remunerated?

ISABELLE. Why did you send me to Arthur Beale?

ASTRID. Is that what this is about?

ISABELLE. I can't think why you would want to punish me.

ASTRID. Punish you? What did he do?

ISABELLE. Do you care?

ASTRID. You say the boundaries aren't clear? Then let's make them crystal. I pay for your time. Sometimes I want to eat steak, sometimes I want you to see a friend, and sometimes I want to sit on your face – regardless, your time is paid for. If you are displeased with this arrangement, then talk to me about it in a professional manner. As for Arthur Beale specifically, if he's mistreated you, yes, I care, because it now taints our relationship. So, again, what did he do?

ISABELLE. Why did you send me?

ASTRID. Because I thought he would like you! And it's in my interests to make Arthur happy, to look on me favourably.

ISABELLE. You sent me to that fucking sadist because you wanted me demeaned.

ASTRID. How do you demean a whore? I'm seriously asking here, how?

Beat.

ISABELLE *gets up to leave.*

Come on, you're walking out? Do we really need these theatrics?

ISABELLE. Consider our professional relationship terminated.

ASTRID. A grand. It's yours. For whatever went wrong with Arthur. Compensation. Sit down, let's finish our dinner.

ISABELLE. You really don't understand anyone, do you? It's not about money.

ASTRID. Fine, two grand, done, let's eat.

ISABELLE. I wouldn't see you again if you paid me ten
thousand! This is the truth about you, Astrid. You aren't
a human being – you're just an approximation of one. If you
weren't such a cunt, I'd feel sorry for you. Cos what you're
too dumb to realise is that I'm the closest you'll ever be to
loving anyone, I'm the only thing that helps you pass for
vaguely real at all.

ASTRID. Your real name's Tina Brown. You're from Bum-fuck
Midlands nowhere, but you've worked hard to lose that accent
and if I don't listen too closely I could almost believe you
were privately educated in the south. You married a French
teacher, then left after a year. Your nine-year-old daughter
from a previous relationship, father unknown – Mia, is it? –
lives with the teacher still. They haven't heard from you in a
while. Mia wishes you would call.

Beat.

How can you make me real? You're one hundred per cent
genuine phoney.

ISABELLE *puts her hand on* ASTRID'*s cheek, a gesture of
compassion that throws* ASTRID *completely.*

ISABELLE. You're such a fool, Astrid, such a stupid stupid fool.

ISABELLE *gathers her things to leave.*

ASTRID. Ten thousand. Okay, I'll give you ten thousand.
A gesture of good faith.

WAITER *hands* ISABELLE *her coat.*

You'll never have to see Arthur again, you'll never have to
see anyone.

ISABELLE *puts on her scarf and gloves.*

Don't be an idiot. This is pride, fuck pride, okay? It's ten
thousand, think of what that could mean for you, think of
what it could mean to… to Mia, think of Mia –

ISABELLE *grabs the steak knife and puts it to* ASTRID'*s
throat. The action is fast.*

ISABELLE. If you even say my daughter's name, if you even think it –

I will kill you before I let you own me. You think you're hard? You have no idea who I am and what I've done and what I can still do.

ISABELLE *lowers the knife and* ASTRID *holds up her hand to indicate to the* WAITER *that she is okay, that everything is okay.*

ISABELLE *leaves.*

Twelve

A nightclub.

PRIYA *is holding court with* JEAN-PIERRE *(a Swiss national) and a group of* MEN IN SUITS.

They're all pretty drunk and loose.

She shuffles a deck of cards, showing an impressive display of shuffling technique: weaving, riffling, pharaoh shuffle, etc.

PRIYA.... so two potatoes walk into a bar. And the first potato is a little sore about how the second potato is treating him so the first potato says to the second potato, 'Why do you skin me like that?'

ASTRID *enters but no one notices.*

And the second potato says to the first potato, 'You could say... cos it's a-peeling.'

Everyone groans, laughing.

PRIYA *'badoom-chings' then shows* JEAN-PIERRE *the Queen of Diamonds.*

Was this your card?

JEAN-PIERRE. Unbelievable!

SUIT 1. How d'you do that?

SUIT 2. Seriously, that's fucking amazing!

SUIT 1. You're cheating, right? Tell me you're cheating, what's the trick?

PRIYA. Tricks is what a hooker does for a twenty. I'm performing magic.

PRIYA *shuffles cards again.*

Pick a card, any card.

SUIT 1 *picks a card.*

I want you to remember that card. Can you do that for me?

SUIT 1. Anything for you.

PRIYA *winks as she shuffles the deck.*

PRIYA. So what do you call a grenade thrown in a kitchen? Linoleum Blown-apart.

Everyone groans again but PRIYA *has them in the palm of her hand.*

Two hats hang on a couple of hooks in the hallway. One hat says to the other, 'You stay here. I'll go on ahead.'

ASTRID. So what's the game? Shit puns and two-dollar card tricks?

JEAN-PIERRE. Astrid!

JEAN-PIERRE *and* ASTRID *kiss hello.*

PRIYA. Boys, this is Astrid Wentworth, the best bookie in the City.

SUIT 2. Hi, Astrid.

SUIT 1. *Enchanté, mademoiselle.*

SUIT 2. Drink?

JEAN-PIERRE. You've been hiding this one away, haven't you?

ASTRID. Have I?

PRIYA *shows the deck of cards.*

PRIYA. Was this your card?

SUIT 1. How'd you do that? How?

SUIT 2. This is black magic!

SUIT 1. She's a black devil woman!

ASTRID. Jean-Pierre, tell me how was –

JEAN-PIERRE. And you get to sit next to her every day?

ASTRID. Sorry?

SUIT 1. Do another!

SUIT 2. Give us a joke!

SUIT 1. Watch her hands, it's all distraction!

　　PRIYA *shuffles the cards.*

PRIYA. There's a soldier, right? He's seen it all. He's survived mustard gas, he's survived pepper spray, he's a true seasoned veteran.

SUIT 2. That's fucking shit!

SUIT 1. Terrible, appalling!

SUIT 2. Seasoned veteran!

ASTRID. Sorry I couldn't make dinner but –

JEAN-PIERRE. Priya looked after me, didn't you, Priya?

PRIYA. Jean-Pierre's been good enough to pretend to be amused by my pathetic jokes –

JEAN-PIERRE. They're not just pathetic, they're shit!

PRIYA. The worst!

ASTRID. A woman of many talents, our Priya. And secrets. I didn't know you could do... cards.

PRIYA. There was a talent show when I was fifteen and I can't sing and I can't dance so I grift. Is this your card?

　　PRIYA *cuts the deck and holds up a card.*

SUIT 1. No!

SUIT 2. Ha!

SUIT 1. In your face!

ASTRID. Oh well, so, Jean-Pierre –

PRIYA. Dear me. I don't understand. I really thought…
Wherever could your card be? Have you checked your
pocket?

SUIT 1. No fucking way…

SUIT 2. Is it?

SUIT 1. Don't tell me…?

SUIT 1 *checks his pocket. He finds the Nine of Clubs.*

SUIT 2. I don't fucking believe it!

SUIT 1. She's good!

SUIT 2. The girl is good!

PRIYA. Thank you. Thank you.

JEAN-PIERRE. Speaking of cards, your dance card is full these
days, no, Astrid?

ASTRID. What do you mean by that?

JEAN-PIERRE. Morgan Stanley is a big fish.

ASTRID. Big fish aren't always the tastiest, Jean-Pierre. You
know that.

JEAN-PIERRE. Still, all the same, you're a busy woman,
maybe too busy for UBS.

ASTRID. Never too busy for –

JEAN-PIERRE. How'd you feel if I let young Priya handle my
business?

ASTRID. You want Priya?

JEAN-PIERRE. She can't do it?

ASTRID. She's very good, of course. In fact, I was hoping you
two would hit it off –

JEAN-PIERRE. So it's okay with you?

ASTRID. I was going to suggest Priya become more directly
involved with your account. I just wasn't sure you'd be so
keen for a junior –

JEAN-PIERRE. I like to help people come up in the business.

ASTRID. So good of you to take a chance on new talent. I have to admit I'm a little hurt you're so keen to drop me! We've had a relationship for –

JEAN-PIERRE. Donkey's years so they say. I remember you before Botox! That's how old I am!

ASTRID. Careful, Jean-Pierre, tread lightly, light footsteps –

JEAN-PIERRE. Come on, Astrid, you've blown me off the past two times. How much rejection can a man stand before he takes the hint?

ASTRID. Nothing could be further from the truth! You are my top priority, Jean-Pierre, you always –

JEAN-PIERRE. There's no hard feelings, I understand. You have bigger fish now. So give me to the smaller fisherman, yes? I like being the biggest fish.

ASTRID. This couldn't have worked out more perfectly. I'll oversee her personally.

JEAN-PIERRE. I like being a young girl's first.

ASTRID. Jean-Pierre, you filthy fuck.

PRIYA *shuffles cards and grins at* ASTRID.

ASTRID *smiles back, albeit more forced.*

Thirteen

A cabaret nightclub.

ASTRID *and* PRIYA *sing Rosemary Clooney and Vera Ellen's 'Sisters'.*

Fourteen

A masked ball.

BOOKIES, PRIYA, HARRISON *and* ASTRID *are at a masked ball wearing animal masks. Everyone is already shitfaced. Someone isn't wearing trousers.*

ASTRID *is on her third martini, while* PRIYA *and* HARRISON *are downing a row of tequila shots. The object of the game is to finish their shots first...*

BOOKIES. Drink drink drink drink drink!

> PRIYA *finishes her last shot and slams it on the bar, to much raucous cheering.*

PRIYA. In your face, Ralph! You fucking pussy!

> *More raucous cheering.*

> HARRISON *is trying not to gag.*

ASTRID (*scanning the room*). There's not a single worthwhile person here.

BOOKIE 1. It's like an *Eyes Wide Shut* party, and you can have filthy faeces fisting sex and it's alright cos you're wearing a mask and no one knows who's fisting who.

> ASTRID *stares at the unmasked* BOOKIE.

BOOKIE 2. Some fucking penis wrinkle is seeing how many lengths he can swim underwater! He's about to get in the pool.

ASTRID. Let's hope no one drowns or we'll be short a client in the morning.

BOOKIE 1. See that guy? See that guy? Saw him dancing once butt-naked to 50 Cent. Swear to god, cock out and everything. And then he put his glasses on his cock and sort of swung it like a sock puppet.

BOOKIE 2. Awesome.

BOOKIE 1. You seen Franklin's Lamborghini?

PRIYA. You been eating a cowpat? What the fuck is on your face?

BOOKIE 1. Chocolate. From the chocolate fountain. Y'know what? Let's smear chocolate on it. Let's smear chocolate on Franklin's Lamborghini. It'll be funny cos it'll look like shit.

BOOKIE 1 *and* PRIYA *rush out.*

HARRISON, BOOKIE 2, *and* ASTRID *stay.*

BOOKIE 2. Anyone here you haven't fucked?

ASTRID. Monday I screw Morgan Stanley; Tuesday it's HSBC; Wednesday Swiss Capital; Thursday JP Morgan; Friday I work with my physio on my vaginal muscles, all that repetitive stress injury. That's why I have a client list that you can only wank into your socks over. Cos I'm just so good at fucking.

BOOKIE 2 *laughs.*

BOOKIE 2. How you feel about the kid? Sengupta. The new T&A on the block. Y'know, the one that's not menopausal.

ASTRID. I know this is difficult for you, given that your only understanding of female interaction is scratching each other's eyes out which you think inevitably leads to sex. But my protégée's success is my success. Sengupta is the best junior in the firm by a long way.

No one acknowledges that HARRISON *is within earshot.*

God you're all so fucking boring. This is a waste of my time.

ASTRID *leaves.*

BOOKIE 2 (*to* HARRISON). 'Sengupta's the best junior in the firm.' Does it hurt? Everyone thinking you're nobody?

HARRISON *doesn't respond.*

Y'know Astrid's protected her from the beginning? Told the whole floor that if anyone fucked with the kid she'd destroy them.

HARRISON. Astrid did that?

BOOKIE 2. You've been walking round with a bull's-eye on your back and the girl got a free ride. How well d'you think she'd be doing if Ian dipped his balls in her water glass?

HARRISON. Has Ian dipped his balls in my water glass?

BOOKIE 2. Every day.

Beat.

You fucked her?

HARRISON. Astrid?

BOOKIE 2. The kid. Jesus Christ, Ralph, keep up. I fucked
a curry once. Regular smell but they kinda taste different,
like coriander, or lamb or something. Y'know more spicy.
The Karma Sutra's Indian.

HARRISON. My dad says, never sleep with a woman in the
business. Because if she survives, she's going to have real
power. Because she's had to work so much harder, she's had
to be so much tougher. So don't fuck up those relationships
with... fucking.

BOOKIE 2. You're the most dickless man I've ever met.
You've no dick, right? Tell me, c'mon, just say it, say,
'I have no dick.'

HARRISON. I don't know how to respond to that.

BOOKIE 2. Prove me wrong, you fucking suppository! I used
to play football and my coach would say, 'Put away the
Rohypnol, boys, buy her two Long Island Iced Teas, same
result and it's legal.'

HARRISON *doesn't understand.*

She's so fucking pissed she'd let a rhino do her, with its horn.

HARRISON *shakes his head.*

HARRISON. I don't think so, it's not –

BOOKIE 2. Fuck me! Brainwave! FaceTime me!

HARRISON. What?

BOOKIE 2. When you're fucking Sengupta! I did this once at
uni with this really fat chick I pulled. Fucking funny as. She
was going down on me in the toilets and I FaceTimed my
mates out in the bar –

HARRISON. What?

HARRISON *is drunk, unsteady and trying to leave.*

BOOKIE 1 *stumbles back in laughing, chocolate over his hands, and corners* HARRISON.

BOOKIE 1. So here's a pair of fags, what you two been up to then? Bumming?

BOOKIE 2. Where's Sengupta?

BOOKIE 1. I dunno, taking a piss, why?

BOOKIE 2. Stevenson here is gonna fuck her!

BOOKIE 1. Who's Stevenson? Holy fuck, you mean Ralph?!

BOOKIE 2. Stevenson's gonna FaceTime it!

BOOKIE 1. No fucking way, Stevenson!

BOOKIE 2. Thatta boy, Stevenson!

HARRISON. I'm not going to –

BOOKIE 1. That would be the most amazing thing I've ever seen! And I've got a video of this huge black man with the face of Alicia Silverstone bumming this MILF – and this would be more amazing than that and that's pretty fucking amazing!

BOOKIE 2. Didn't think you had it in you, son!

HARRISON. I'm not –

BOOKIE 2. Just take her to those loos and FaceTime me, couldn't be easier, you FaceTime me –

HARRISON. This is crazy, I'm not –

BOOKIE 1. We'll have to come up with a new nickname.

HARRISON. A new nickname? For me?

BOOKIE 2. Libertine Lover?

BOOKIE 1. Smooth Operator?

BOOKIE 2. Martin? As in Scorsese, because of the filmmaking thing?

BOOKIE 1. Or we stick with Dickless

BOOKIE 2. Dickless

BOOKIE 1. On account of you having no dick

HARRISON. I've got a… I've got a dick

BOOKIE 1. No, you don't

BOOKIE 2. That's why we call you dickless

BOOKIE 1. Dickless Dickless

Everyone takes up the chant.

BOOKIES. Dickless Dickless Dickless Dickless Dickless Dickless Dickless Dickless Dickless Dickless–

The chanting continues as HARRISON *tries to be heard.*

HARRISON. I'm not going to do it because you guys keep calling me –

PRIYA. Dickless?

PRIYA is unsteady on her feet.

Everyone holds their breath, unsure of what she has heard.

Dickless? Dickless?

PRIYA bursts out laughing at HARRISON.

Y'know what Ralph wants to be when he grows up?

HARRISON. Priya, don't –

PRIYA. He wants to be a comedian and he's gonna tell stories about us, about all of us… because he thinks he's funny!

Everyone bursts out laughing.

BOOKIE 1. Tell us a joke, Dickless! Do me!

BOOKIE 2. Be funny, Dickless! Go on, be funny!

BOOKIE 1. Do your impression of me! Do me! Do me!

PRIYA. Dickless! Because you have no dick, Ralph!

HARRISON downs a shot and kisses PRIYA.

This takes everyone by surprise – PRIYA *kisses back.*

Enormous cheering as PRIYA *and* HARRISON *stumble out of the bar into the toilets.*

Fifteen

A cabaret club.

ASTRID *sings the first verse of Nina Simone's 'Do I Move You?'*

ASTRID. The most crucial element in sex... is lighting. Know
your angles, work the shadows. Missionary obviously gives
you the flatter stomach but it also means your thighs spread
and your breasts fall into your armpits.

She sings the second verse.

We look better on top and men prefer us there, they can see
more, feel more, do less. Every woman must be a skilled
contortionist. You've got to suck in your stomach, thrust
your hips, arch your back, stick your arse out, all at the same
time – it hurts, but the pain can really help with your pout,
which he'll read as something urgent, animalistic, like a
Guernica horse cumming really hard.

She sings the third verse.

Can I let you in on a little secret? Something I've never told
anyone.

I've fucked a lot of men, a LOT of men and the truth is... if
it's an orgasm I want, I've got my Lelo Siri Luxury
Rechargeable Clitoral Vibrator (black, obviously). I don't
have sex with men to cum, I have sex to win. Winning is
them wanting something from you, and the key is to be so
good at it they want it from you again, and again, and again.
That's the fundamental of all power dynamics – have
something they want. If you don't, you've got bupkis, baby.
Who doesn't want to be a sex symbol? Who doesn't want
a twenty-three-inch waist and better tits? Who doesn't want
to be wanted?

She sings the last refrain.

A woman's body is an instrument – play it like fucking
Stravinsky.

Sixteen

Peterson Jones & Walker office.

PRIYA. I'm going to the police.

ASTRID. You don't want to do that.

PRIYA. But I do want / to do that –

ASTRID. You will not fucking talk to the fucking police.

Beat.

PRIYA. I hoped... I thought you might come with me.

ASTRID. I'm responsible for you, right? You are on your way because of me. You will not embarrass me with this bullshit prank.

PRIYA. A prank?

ASTRID. No one put a gun to your head. You were sucking back tequila like it was... ideological, like you had a cause, like each shot wipes off ten mil of third-world debt.

PRIYA. You told me to drink! You told me I had to fit in! You pressured me into, / everyone pressured me to –

ASTRID. Then we need to work on your alcohol tolerance.

Beat.

You drank too much, okay, shit happens. Things transpired... you wish they hadn't. Hell, that's my entire relationship history. Laugh it off.

PRIYA. Laugh it off? That's your advice?

ASTRID. Paris Hilton released three sex tapes and got a fucking Guess modelling contract, okay? I'm just suggesting that perhaps there's a bigger picture here, it's a question of perspective. You could walk back into that office right now a fucking cucumber, cool as shit, nothing to apologise for, nothing to be embarrassed about, so you got pissed and fucked a guy on camera, so fucking what?

PRIYA. I was raped.

ASTRID. You'll never work in the City again.

PRIYA. And he... showed it to people, they saw it, I remember he had the phone but I thought he was... I don't know what, I blacked out before... and they were watching it, they're laughing about it, like it's funny, like me being raped is funny.

ASTRID. Listen to me, Priya, very carefully. They'll have at least ten witnesses to say that you were fucked off your tits on alcohol, cocaine, ketamine –

PRIYA. I've never taken drugs in my life –

ASTRID. The truth doesn't fucking matter! Every email you've ever sent, every email you've received, your phone messages, everything, they will scan it all and they will find something to paint you as a nymphomaniac, drug-addled, drunk freak whore. Worse, they'll say you're a shit bookie and you've only invented this incident to cover your professional incompetence. They will destroy you, utterly. I'm not threatening you – this is not a threat. I'm simply telling you what will happen. I'm giving you the data.

PRIYA. I was fucking raped!

Beat.

ASTRID. Let's not use... the 'R' word, okay, let's not get all inflammatory –

PRIYA. What would you / call it?

ASTRID. Why were you in the toilets with him? What did you think would happen? Were you hoping to discuss the finer points of Proust?

PRIYA. I passed out. I don't remember how I got there. Just that I woke up on the floor, my thighs smeared with... I wasn't fucking conscious! How can I consent if I wasn't fucking conscious?

ASTRID. Priya, I understand that you've... been quite sheltered. It's a religious thing, a cultural thing, whatever. But what happened last night, it happens all the time. You had sex. Bad, drunk, passed-out sex... Jesus, I've never had sex sober.

PRIYA. You're telling me to shrug off rape like it's a bad haircut –

ASTRID. Stop fucking using the 'R' word!

They stare at each other.

PRIYA. Rape.

ASTRID. If you were a man and you had messy sex you couldn't remember, you would laugh about this. This would be an anecdote. Waking up somewhere you don't recognise, awkward conversation with their housemate as you fish in the larder for Nurofen. This would be funny. Instead, you're acting like a fucking female from 1853 and your poor honour has been besmirched. We can have sex now.

PRIYA. Rape.

ASTRID. That's playing the woman card. It's hands in the air surrender, it's you squealing at the top of your girlish lungs 'I can't take it in boys' world' and there goes the authority on which your job and career depends.

PRIYA. I'm so stupid. I actually thought… you cared about me, that we were friends.

ASTRID. This is how it is, Priya. So put on your big-girl pants and grow the fuck up.

The two look at each other until ASTRID *looks away.*

Seventeen

Peterson Jones & Walker office.

A document lies between ARTHUR *and* PRIYA.

PRIYA. I'm not signing it.

ARTHUR. And I don't want you to. Not until you're sure that's what you want.

PRIYA. I was raped by Harrison Stevenson. I'm not pretending it didn't happen.

ARTHUR. If you'd like me to come with you to the police station, of course, I'll be there.

PRIYA. You will?

ARTHUR. We're a family here at Peterson Jones and Walker.
I know we work hard and we're uncouth and we say terrible
things to each other, part of the rough and tumble of
business, of stress, but that's how family is – messy and
rude. But if something happens to one of our own… it
happens to all of us.

PRIYA. You've never even spoken to me before. You don't
know I exist. And we all know who Harrison Stevenson's
father is. So this preamble about how you're on my side?
Why don't you say what you want to say?

ARTHUR. Miss Sengupta, I don't blame you for thinking…
a little cynically about me. My job is to make things work.
However I do that, whatever it takes, I make sure the
currencies team in this company is the envy of the City.
We have the biggest clients, the highest volume of trades,
and to put it crudely, make more cash than any other
brokerage in London. I'm proud of that reputation and feel
I, in my own small way, have helped build it. You're right in
assuming that I would do a great many things to protect that
reputation, and myself. But you're wrong if you think I need
to play you, need to orchestrate some outcome.

Let me explain to you how things work. If you go to the
police, and I'll support you whatever decision you make, but
if you go, I get bollocked by my bosses for letting my shop
get out of order. They may demote me, they may take it out
on my bonus, I might even be sacked. There'll be newspaper
articles, media attention, opinion pieces about sexism in the
City, how we need a culture change. There may be a TV
news panel featuring a feminist academic with a silver bob.
And the PR agents of my bosses' bosses will need to work a
little harder. Harrison Stevenson will be sacked, as he must
be, and his father will take his bank's business elsewhere.
And the business of PJW, by and large, goes on as normal.
There are other clients, new trades, and the sun will always
come up tomorrow. These are all perfectly forseeable events.
What's less forseeable is what happens to you.

PRIYA. That's a threat.

ARTHUR. Not remotely. It's the truth. Will you still want to
work here? If not, where will you work? How will this affect

the relationships you have with clients now and in future?
Do you want to be known as the girl who cried rape? This is
not a threat. This is me asking questions I don't know the
answer to. And unless you're an oracle, you don't know
those answers either.

PRIYA. So the only person I hurt is myself, right? I should just
pretend I wasn't raped, like I'm supposed to walk into the
office every day and say, 'Morning, arseholes, who do I have
to fuck to get a decent cup of coffee in this city?'

ARTHUR. You should do no such thing. Harrison Stevenson is
a despicable little worm, and worse, a bad bookie. He's gone,
eliminated, effective immediately.

PRIYA. But his dad –

ARTHUR. His dad is a client, not god. Fuck him.

PRIYA. He should be in prison. What he did –

ARTHUR. Do you know what happens if you go to the police?
It becomes about you, not him. You were drinking, you
voluntarily went off with him. You were going to have
consensual sex with Harrison Stevenson – that's the story
everyone will hear.

PRIYA. I was unconscious.

ARTHUR. Says you. He'll say how much you wanted him, how
you tried to unzip him in the corridor, et cetera.

PRIYA. There are witnesses who saw I was unconscious. That's
what makes it so hilarious.

ARTHUR. Witnesses are unreliable. It was dark, they were
drunk, the image was shaky, the screen small. I'm sorry,
Miss Sengupta, but getting a rape conviction is as rare as a
winning lottery ticket.

PRIYA. So whatever I do, he gets away with it?

ARTHUR. That's the way of the world, Miss Sengupta.

Beat.

Forget about him losing. Focus on you winning. Where do
you see yourself in five years?

PRIYA. You can't be serious. You want me to outline my career goals? Am I supposed to use this 'opportunity' to pitch for lines?

ARTHUR. Why not?

PRIYA *is thrown*.

PRIYA. You'll give me lines to keep me quiet?

ARTHUR. You've earned the right to greater responsibilities because of your excellent work. Astrid tells me you're an outstanding junior and I believe in investing in talent. So tell me… what is it you want?

Beat.

PRIYA. What about the ones who watched it? What happens to them?

ARTHUR. What do you want to happen? You want them gone? They're gone.

PRIYA. I want them annihilated.

ARTHUR. How do you propose we do that?

PRIYA. Please don't patronise me, Arthur. Please don't pretend you don't know what I'm talking about. A phone call from you to the right people in the right places and they'll never work in the City again. I want them cleaning toilets at Burger King.

Beat.

ARTHUR. It can be arranged, Miss Sengupta, it can be arranged.

PRIYA. And Astrid?

ARTHUR. What about Astrid?

PRIYA. She threatened me. Told me to keep my mouth shut or else I'd never work again.

ARTHUR. Astrid's a terrific bookie.

PRIYA. With terrific lines.

ARTHUR. You want me to give you Astrid's lines? I want to help you out, Miss Sengupta, you show real promise but you're twenty-three years old. I'm not giving you Morgan Stanley.

PRIYA. You're not giving me anything. Like you said, I've earned it. Jacob Vibert wants a woman to handle his business. He likes hearing our voice cut through the testosterone over the box.

ARTHUR. And he's got a woman. He's got Astrid. I'm not shit-canning her because you're brawling for a catfight.

PRIYA. You're shit-canning her because I was raped and she did nothing! Not a fucking thing!

ARTHUR. You're only here because Astrid took a chance on you.

PRIYA. And I have been grateful. I've inputted her tickets, booked her restaurants, picked up her dry-cleaning, bought her four-shot skim-milk lattes – I have been the best fucking junior you could want. I'm done with being grateful to Astrid Wentworth.

Beat.

ARTHUR. I'll take fifty per cent of your bro on Morgan Stanley. This isn't negotiation – that's the cost. Take it or leave it.

ARTHUR *offers* PRIYA *a pen and pushes the document closer to her.*

PRIYA *takes the pen but before she signs…*

PRIYA. I want to be here when you tell her, I want to see Astrid's face.

Beat.

ARTHUR *nods.*

PRIYA *signs.*

ARTHUR. Well done, Miss Sengupta. Very well played.

PRIYA. I'm not playing.

ARTHUR. Of course not.

ARTHUR *beckons* ASTRID *into his office.*

We've been talking, Miss Sengupta and I, and she is satisfied that we can handle this matter in-house.

ASTRID *is noticeably relieved.*

ASTRID (*to* PRIYA). You're making the right choice, the smart choice.

ARTHUR. This is what happened. You, Priya Sengupta, Harrison Stevenson and others were drinking. You encouraged Miss Sengupta to drink more than she was comfortable with. Miss Sengupta became intoxicated. You coerced Mr Stevenson into pursuing her sexually for the purpose of filming it. It was an appalling joke in the worst possible taste, for which, you take full responsibility.

ASTRID. Priya, what have you done? Priya –

ARTHUR. DID I SAY SPEAK?

Uncomfortable silence.

Let me make this abundantly clear. You're finished. I mean forever and ever. In totality. For the rest of time. I mean, you couldn't trade yak's milk out of a Mongolian yurt if you had all the abacuses in Central Asia – that's how fucking finished you are.

ASTRID. I'll tell your wife about Isabelle.

ARTHUR. I beg your fucking pardon?

ASTRID. Beverley might be very interested in knowing about you fucking whores.

Beat.

ARTHUR. Listen to me, you cunt, you don't want to play with me.

ASTRID. No, you don't want to play with me.

Pause.

ARTHUR *picks up the phone, dials, puts it on speakerphone.*

MRS BEALE (*speakerphone*). Hello?

ARTHUR. Beverley, it's Arthur.

MRS BEALE (*speakerphone*). Is this on speakerphone?

ARTHUR. You remember Astrid Wentworth?

MRS BEALE (*speakerphone*). That woman in your department?

ARTHUR. She gave me a prostitute to fuck. And I fucked her. We'll talk about it later.

ARTHUR *hangs up*.

That it, sweetheart? Is that all you've got? Word to the wise, darling, when you're trying to fuck someone, you better be holding something more potent than a face like a slapped arse.

ASTRID. Priya, say something. Tell him the truth, I didn't –

PRIYA. The truth doesn't matter.

ASTRID. I brought you in here. I hired you, I vouched for you –

PRIYA. And you lost to me.

Beat.

ASTRID. What did you give her?

ARTHUR. Just your lines.

ASTRID (*to* ARTHUR). You made her sign a gagging clause, right? She can never disclose what happened. Poor kid thinks she's won when all you've done is kept her close so you can fuck her worse. You bastard, Arthur.

PRIYA. I'm not stupid! They can't terminate my contract for at least two years which is much more than I need to prove how valuable I –

ASTRID. Clients won't take your calls, tip-offs won't come through, deals just never fall your way – he'll make sure of it, won't you, Arthur? You won't be a broker but a eunuch. You signed your own death warrant and you don't even know it.

PRIYA *tries to make sense of this*.

Fuck you, Arthur.

ARTHUR. Adios, Miss Wentworth.

ARTHUR *leaves*.

PRIYA. I was raped. I was unconscious and he raped me. And they watched it. And they laughed about it. Like it was… like I don't exist. And you wanted me, you wanted me –

ASTRID. To survive.

PRIYA. I don't want to just survive, I want to fucking win!

ASTRID. They always win, they always win.

PRIYA. So what are we playing for?

ASTRID kisses the cheek of a confused PRIYA.

ASTRID. To keep playing a little longer.

Eighteen

A hotel bar.

ISABELLE *sits at the bar.*

ASTRID *sits beside her.* ISABELLE *makes to leave but* ASTRID *holds her arm.*

ASTRID. Please.

ISABELLE. I don't want to see you, Astrid.

ASTRID. Please.

Beat.

I don't mean to hijack you like this but you give me little choice. You won't answer my calls – what am I supposed to do?

ASTRID *drains a martini.*

How's business?

ISABELLE. I'm not doing this. I won't sit here and chat and pretend to be your friend. No.

ASTRID *puts money into* ISABELLE*'s hands –* ISABELLE *tries to reject it when she clocks the desperation in* ASTRID*'s face.*

Business is… fine. You?

ASTRID. Thinking of taking a break. I've only had two weeks off in seven years. I want to see the sun.

ISABELLE. You should. You look terrible.

ASTRID. I call it City Grey.

ISABELLE. Y'know that song – (*Sings the tune of 'New York, New York'*.) '…if I can make it there, I'll make it, anywhere, and here's to you…' y'know that song? Always liked that song until I really heard the lyrics, really heard them. And the thing is, why d'you want live in a city where you have to make it? Why not just… live?

ASTRID. Come with me.

ISABELLE. I'm working now, Astrid, I don't –

ASTRID. No, I mean to the sun. Let's go to Barbados. I want to take you to Barbados. First-class airfares, five-star hotel, infinity pools, the works, the absolute works. Let me take you.

ISABELLE. You've never seen me in daylight.

ASTRID. I want to. I'd pay you. I mean I'd pay for everything and pay you. Ten grand for the week. On top of everything else I'll buy.

ISABELLE. I told you. Right at the beginning that I wouldn't save you. I meant it.

ISABELLE *leaves*.

ASTRID *is heartbroken*.

Nineteen

A cabaret club.

ASTRID *sings the first verse and chorus of Etta James' 'I'd Rather Go Blind'.*

ASTRID. Backstory. This is the part of the show where I share an anecdote about childhood, something formative, something that explains me and why I am the person I am today – which is obviously fabulous but damaged. Ooh, we love damaged women, don't we? There is nothing more delicious than a sexy woman who was molested by her uncle, am I right? You know what I'm talking about, you know. She wears her sexuality so obviously, a leopard-print boob-tube synthetic skin, it's so present, all oozing, all needing. She sneaks out of home and goes down on the whole football team, she drinks in car parks with drunks and degenerates, the mothers of nice girls don't let their daughters play with her. She's still that little girl, made to feel dirty and worthless and she desperately desperately needs you to save her, to make her whole. But alas, you can't save her, no one can. She's on a one-way ticket to self-destruction. Which is, to be honest, for the best really because can you imagine living with Marilyn Monroe? Really? Vulnerability is fine as long as there's an end point otherwise it's just fucking annoying. Tell me I'm beautiful, tell me I'm pretty, tell me I'm smart, tell me you love me, tell me you love me, love me love me love me love me love me. You want the warm and fuzzies of trying to save someone who can't be saved, without the responsibility.

So here's my anecdote, here's me being vulnerable, the scared little kid behind the bitch façade, no longer an object of hate but pity. Here goes.

I had a dog. Pearl. Strangest fucking dog you ever saw – part Jack Russell, part Staffie, part dachshund and the worst case of ringworm the vet had ever seen so she was bald. It was like you took parts of other bald dogs and squished them together and that was Pearl, short legs, stout long body, curved spine. The bitch had personality and I loved her. But she had a fart on her that would stun a donkey. Truly. You'd be watching television and the smell was so ripe, you know when it's so thick, you can taste shit in your mouth?

And my father would say, choking a little on his own vomit, one of these days, Pearl, one of these days. And then one of these days, Pearl, she was sleeping and she lets out a massive fart, I'm talking the kind of fart that in 1945 you could've flown her over Hiroshima and Nagasaki and she would've got the job done, and my father, choking a little on his own vomit, takes her by the collar, out into the yard, and puts three bullets in her head.

Meaningful pause.

That obviously didn't happen. Obviously, that didn't happen. My father's an accountant, my mother's an ophthalmologist, they're still happily married, they have two golden retrievers – Scaramouche and Indiana Jones (I know) – they live on a lovely property, a former piggery in the country, my mother is part of the Ophthalmologists' Women's Choir, I don't know that there's a huge demand for their music but she's having fun, and my father's redoing the garden. Do I look vulnerable to you? Did you want my father to kill my flatulent dog?

She sings the second verse.

So I find myself in a bar last night… alone and I'm thinking there's boys' world and there's girls' world and you're mistaken if you think you can move between them. Whatever entry points you find, whatever visa you think you're holding, know that the time you spend in boys' world is only temporary. My five-year-old self understood what my adult self had forgotten… they never ever forget that you've got a vagina. They never ever forget your true place.

She sings the last chorus.

Fuck it, don't go crying into your limited-edition Chanel handbag.

The End.

A Nick Hern Book

Boys Will Be Boys first published in Great Britain in 2016 as a paperback original by Nick Hern Books Limited, The Glasshouse, 49a Goldhawk Road, London W12 8QP, in association with the Bush Theatre, London, and Headlong

Front cover: photography by Olivia Rutherford; design by Well Made

Designed and typeset by Nick Hern Books, London
Printed in Great Britain by CPI Group UK (Ltd)

A CIP catalogue record for this book is available from the British Library

ISBN 978 1 84842 568 2